malta 1565

last battle of the crusades

TIM PICKLES

malta 1565

last battle of the crusades

Praeger Illustrated Military History Series

PRAEGER

Westport, Connecticut
London

Library of Congress Cataloging-in-Publication Data

Pickles, Tim.

    Malta 1565: last battle of the Crusades / Tim Pickles

        p. cm. – (Praeger illustrated military history series, ISSN 1547-206X)

    Originally published: Oxford: Osprey, 1988.

    Includes bibliographical references and index.

    ISBN 0-275-98848-1 (set: alk. paper) – ISBN 0-275-98852-X (alk. paper)

    1. Malta-History – Siege, 1565. I. Title. II. Series

    DG992.6.P53   2005

    945.8'502 – dc22   2005044303

British Library Cataloguing in Publication Data is available.

First published in paperback in 1988 by Osprey Publishing Limited, Midland House, West Way, Botley, Oxford OX2 0HP. All rights reserved.

Copyright © 2005 by Osprey Publishing Limited

Library of Congress Catalog Card Number: 2005044303

ISBN: 0-275-98852-X

ISSN: 1547-206X

Praeger Publishers, 88 Post Road West, Westport, CT 06881

An imprint of Greenwood Publishing Group, Inc.

www.praeger.com

Printed in China through World Print Ltd.

The paper used in this book complies with the Permanent Paper Standard issued by the National Information Standards Organization (Z39.48-1984).

10 9 8 7 6 5 4 3 2 1

ILLUSTRATED BY CHRISTA HOOK

CONTENTS

KEY TO MILITARY SYMBOLS

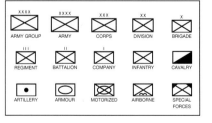

ORIGINS OF THE CAMPAIGN

The immediate cause of what is perhaps the most heroic and (for the defenders) successful siege in history was the necessity of an invading power to clear away a deadly threat to its lines of communication before beginning the campaign that would bring all Europe under the sway of the Ottoman Empire. However, its origins can be traced back to the first time a European army marched to the Holy Land to raise the standard of Christ in the land of the Muslims. That the first Crusaders reached and captured Jerusalem was seen as miraculous, an obvious sign of God's favour, but the excesses of the slaughter in the aftermath were never forgotten nor forgiven by the Muslims.

Outremere, the land across the sea, as the Kingdom of Jerusalem was known, lasted for 200 years and finally fell through a combination of weak kings and ill-advised campaigns in the Holy Land, in a climate of mounting indifference in Europe (**see Warrior 18 *Knight of Outremer***). Along the way, the great Eastern Empire of Byzantium, the bulwark of Christianity, had been undermined, attacked and emasculated by the very forces that had left Europe to defend it and win back the Holy Land. Moreover, the Muslims, who by then dominated the Middle East, fell more and more under the control of warlike descedants of Genghis Khan's Mongols. When the latter had first come from the East, they had been inclined towards Christianity but had been won over by European indifference and Muslim single-mindedness. A mix of the old intellectual pursuits, faith and with new militaristic fanaticism was creating a fearsome empire. Europe's jugular vein was bared.

In the early days of the Kingdom of Jerusalem there was no standing army – a worrying situation in a kingdom surrounded by enemies. Those Knights from Europe who took part in the Crusade and had not found themselves fiefdoms considered their duty done and prepared to return home. This was the background to the formation of the Military and Hospitaller Orders of Knighthood, the first of which was probably the Order of St. John. They were really monks like any others, but they also took on the responsibility of car-

ing for the sick and protecting pilgrims. Over the years they took on distinctive roles. St. Lazarus cared for lepers, and any leprous Knights from any of the other Orders – or indeed secular Knights with leprosy – had to join this Order. The Order of St. Lazarus may even pre-date St. John in its foundation, as it was based on a Leper hospital which pre-dates the first Crusade. However, there is also evidence to suggest that both these organisations were divisions of one Order which was eventually divided into two separate arms. The Order of the Temple was military but also created the first international banking system. This made the Order extremely rich, and eventually it was wiped out by King Philip the Fair of France, who wanted to get his hands on its money. The Teutonic Knights were purely military and tended towards secularism, while the Knights (or Canons) of the Holy Sepulchre were much more religious, with the duty of caring for and protecting the shrine of Our Lord's burial.

When the last Christian forces left Palestine and gave up their toe-hold on Cyprus, only one presence remained in the East, the Order of St. John. This Order had acquired the island of Rhodes and had constructed there one of the finest fortifications in the Mediterranean. While still in the Holy Land, every Knight had to spend time 'on caravan' – quite literally protecting the Christian caravans moving between Jerusalem and the coast or through enemy country. Now they were on an island, and they had turned to ships, protecting Christian vessels sailing the area. However, there were other ships around, in particular the ves-

The Knights' victory over the Ottoman Turks on Malta was widely reported throughout Christendom. It was also celebrated in painting and prints, many of which were produced in Italy. This general view is one of a series illustrating the main events of the Turkish siege, each provided with a lettered key indicating the main features and positions of the opposing sides. Fort St. Elmo is at the upper end of the peninsula in the centre while Grand Harbour is on the right. The Ottoman fleet is concentrated in the inlet to the left of St. Elmo while the main Ottoman base-camp is near the top right-hand corner of this picture. (Via Dr. David Chandler)

sels of the Turkish fleets of Suliman the Magnificent, and the Knights did not hesitate to attack them to gain a share of the rich pickings of the Ottoman Empire.

The 26-year-old Ottoman emperor had finally, he thought, broken the Knights of St. John and of Rhodes. After a long and hard-fought siege he accepted the surrender of the Grand Master of the Order and was magnanimous in victory. He allowed the Knights to take their sacred relics, their banners and arms, get into their galleys and sail away from Rhodes forever into what he believed would be honourable and permanent obscurity. He was to regret this decision.

Suliman now turned his attention to bringing the 'true faith' to Europe on the point of his scimitar, and in spite of some significant setbacks, particularly those inflicted by the brilliant but mentally unstable Prince Vlad Dracul, he was only halted, literally and quite spectacularly, at the walls of Vienna in 1529.

The old Orders that had traditionally been in the forefront of fighting for the faith were in disarray. The Templars had been abolished and St. Lazarus was doing more conventional hospital work in France. Although it was never to completely lose its independence, St. Lazarus was in the stages of becoming virtually a French Royal Order. The Teutonic Knights had almost completed their transformation into a secular order of knighthood, and the Canons of the Holy Sepulchre existed virtually in name only. All this time the Knights of St. John and of Rhodes were wandering around Europe (or at least that part of it not affected by the Reformation) looking for a new home; in 1530 they got one.

The Holy Roman Emperor Charles V realised the threat of the ambitious Suliman and offered the Knights of St. John the archipelago made up of the islands of Gozo, Comino and Malta. By this action he gained a governor for a backwater of the empire and a significant addition to his naval forces. He also came up with a compromise. On Rhodes the Knights had been the sovereign power and the Grand Master had been an independent prince. Charles asked a yearly rent of one falcon from the Knights so that, although they were in practice masters of the islands, answering only to the Pope, they also acknowledged that they held their island from the emperor. No sooner had they taken over the island and its magnificent harbour than they began to harass the Ottoman fleets once more.

Suliman was enraged, and he determined to put right his mistake of showing the Order clemency at the siege of Rhodes.

PLANS AND PREPARATIONS

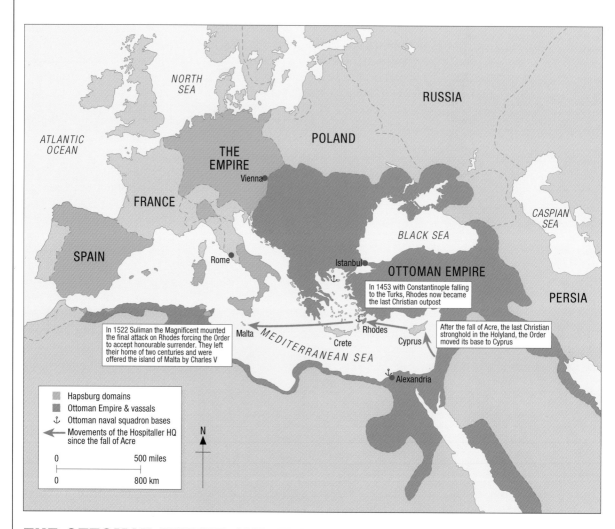

THE OTTOMAN EMPIRE AND THE TRAVELS OF THE ORDER OF ST. JOHN, AD 1200-1564

1 By the beginning of the 13th century the Order had the beginnings of a fleet, mainly used for transportation of supplies and pilgrims. After the fall of Acre, the last Christian stronghold in the Holy Land, the Order moved its base to the island of Cyprus. **2** From Cyprus the Knights used their expanding fleet to raid the mainland. While most of the other Orders began to concentrate their actions on Europe, St. John realised that by expanding it's naval operations could its fight be extended further east. In 1301 the first Admiral was appointed and in 1306 the Order was charged with driving the infidel out of the Byzantine island of Rhodes. By 1307 they had taken several important strongholds and were confirmed as Sovereigns of the island by Pope Clement V, even though it was to be another two years before the last stronghold fell. In 1453 Constantinople fell to the Turks and Rhodes became the last Christian outpost, supported now by its 'Langues' or national jurisdictions in Europe. **3** In 1522 Suliman the Magnificent mounted what was to be the decisive attack on Rhodes forcing the Order's surrender and removal from the island, their home for the past two hundred years. They accepted residence on the island of Malta from Charles V, and here the naval skills developed on Rhodes, combined with the finest harbour in the Mediterranean, made the Order a thorn in the flesh of Turkish trade and their plans for future European expansion, forcing Suliman into action.

The acquisition of Malta as their new home was not the end of the troubles for the Order. When they first arrived, the barren rock dismayed many of the Knights who, along with their Grand Master, remembered well the lush fertile island of Rhodes that they had left. They also remembered how, when Rhodes was captured, in spite of De l'Isle Adam's begging, the Christian monarchs had not helped him recapture it, so they knew they would be on their own in their new home. Only four years after the Order took possession of Malta one of the Order's oldest and most wealthy 'Langues' or divisions fell foul of Renascence politics, when Henry VIII, as part of his break with the Pope, finally abolished the Order in England.

The most important area of the island was, of course, the harbour, and immediately upon their arrival Adam had ordered that the defences of St. Angelo, which guarded the southern side of the harbour and the village of Birgu, be strengthened; likewise the walls of the old capital city, Mdina. There was still hope that a better home would be found for the Order eventually, and for a long while no more was done.

Even La Valette, a member of the council, suggested that Tripoli would be a better head-

Ottoman and Christian soldiers skirmish with each other across a river, each side supported by artillery, as illustrated in the Súleymanname manuscript made in 1558. Here cavalry guard the Turkish flanks, whereas in the siege of Malta cavalry played a very minor role. (Ms. Haz. 1517, Topkapi Lib., Istanbul)

quarters, but this hope was dashed when the city was captured in 1551. In 1552 Juan d'Omedes, who had been Grand Master since 1536, commissioned a survey of the defences from Leo Strozzi, one of the great Renascence captains, and appointed a commission to make recommendations based on the report. As a result a new star fort called St. Michel was built to protect the southern end of Dockyard Creek, setting up a field of crossfire with Fort St. Angelo. A fort was also set up on the end of Mount Sciberras, commanding the entrance to Grand Harbour to the south and the entrance to Marsamuschetto, Malta's other important harbour, to the north. This fort, which was to play such a vital role in the siege, was called St. Elmo.

The famous Muslim corsair Dragut raided the island in 1551 and landed at Marsamuschetto, marching on Birgu and St. Angelo. He was engaged by the Knights on the Marsa lowlands and on Mount Sciberas. Finding the opposition too strong, Dragut cut his losses and withdrew, raiding the island of Gozo to the north (also one of the Knights' possessions) and taking many of the inhabitants off as slaves. A further fort to protect both harbours, which had been considered a good idea, suddenly became a necessity.

Thus St. Elmo was built – on the site of a lighthouse that had existed since Phoenician times. In fact, their name for the island – Maleth – means 'a haven', referring to the harbours. These harbours were the very thing that made the island so attractive to the Knights, and it was a

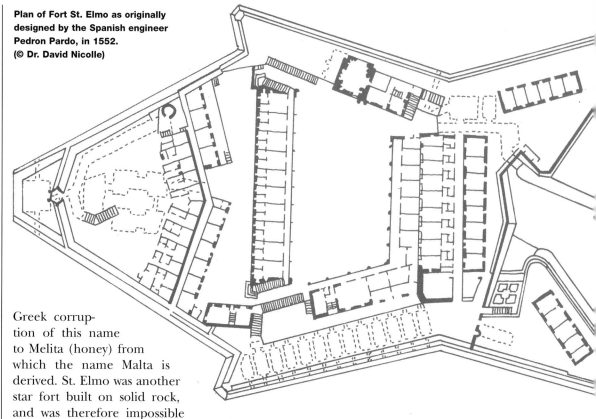

Greek corruption of this name to Melita (honey) from which the name Malta is derived. St. Elmo was another star fort built on solid rock, and was therefore impossible to undermine. However, it was, of necessity, built quickly and was made of sandstone and limestone. These materials were not of the best quality and the internal defences were minimal, mainly through lack of time. In an attempt to counteract this, extensive outworks were built, deep ditches all around, as well as a ravelin facing the heights of mount Sciberas and a cavalier on the northern, seaward side. However, this did not overcome Sciberas's main problem: the heights overlooked the point and provided a ready-made gun platform. In 1557 when La Valette became Grand Master he added a further outwork to St. Elmo; he realised that the cavalier could be approached easily from the Marsamuschetto side. So he constructed a further ravelin of earth and fascines, this work connected to the fort by a narrow fixed bridge and the cavalier by a drawbridge. It is instructive to note that although this last ravelin was built of earth and fascines for speed of construction, all of the materials had to be imported from Sicily, so barren was the island. Unlike lush Rhodes, Malta was going to provide no sustenance to an attacker.

The ships of that attacker appeared almost as the final touches were being added to the last ravelin. Suliman, Sultan of the Ottomans, began preparations in 1564 for an attack on Malta to take place in the spring of 1565. Forty-two years earlier, when he had captured Rhodes, he had said

Fort St. Elmo, from a photograph taken before the second siege by the Germans in World War Two. Although the impressive later fortifications give no idea of the fort that stood during the siege, the importance of the position is well illustrated. This view is taken from the Marsamuschetto side.

LEFT AND BELOW **Two different views of forward sections of the Valetta fortifications, namely St. James Counterguard, Castille Place and St. James Cavalier.**

of the then Grand Master of the Order: "It is not without some pain that I oblige this Christian at his age to leave his home." No such chivalrous thoughts were with him now: the Knights were just an irritant and he wanted to be rid of them.

The Knights had joined King Philip II of Spain in his capture of Penon de la Gomera on the North African coast, a serious blow to Muslim pride but one paid back by the capture of Tripoli by Dragut, who, though a pirate, was a faithful and respected supporter of Suliman. However, the capture of Penon de la Gomera had shown how dangerous the Knights were in Malta. To quote Suliman's advisors: "So long as Malta remains in the hands of the Knights so long will every relief from Constantinople to Tripoli run the danger of being taken or destroyed... This cursed rock is like a barrier interposed between... your possessions. If you will not decide to take it quickly, it will in a short time interrupt all communications between Africa and Asia and the islands of the Archipelago." Even Dragut chipped in: "Until you have smoked out this nest of vipers, you can do no good anywhere." When Dragut spoke, even Suliman would listen.

At Rhodes the Knights had been so close to Constantinople that Suliman had had no difficulty in keeping an eye on them, but from the remote island of

The taste for the exotic is nothing new: here, trained lions are taken through the streets of Istanbul on their way to a grand entertainment for the Sultan. (*Moeurs, Usages et Costumes au Moyen Age*, 1871)

Malta they could strike with their oared galleys at his trading fleets with virtual impunity, while he had almost no knowledge of their intentions. His final spur though was his daughter Mihrmah, by his favourite wife Roxellane. She along with other members of the harem were 'investors' in a venture by Kustir-Aga, chief eunuch of the seraglio of the Sultan, to import luxury goods from Venice. Their ship was captured by perhaps the greatest of the Order's admirals, the Chevalier Romegas, and along with the treasure (valued at 80,000 ducats) several distinguished subjects were captured and held for ransom, including Mihrmah's old nurse. Slaves powered the galleys, and captive Muslims were used by the Knights as captive Christians were used by the Muslims. Now every member of Suliman's harem, led by his daughter and the chief eunuch, was screaming for vengeance, while from the mosques imams cried that true believers were being flogged like dogs at the oars of the galleys in which they were captive. In October 1564 Suliman called a Divan, or grand council.

Considerations other than wounded honour swung the debate as Suliman now realised the strategic importance of Malta. He was told: "There has never been an occasion when they have attacked one of our ships that they have not either sunk or captured it." That threat had to be eliminated, and once captured, Malta's magnificent harbours could be used by the Ottoman fleet to dominate the Mediterranean. From that base, Sicily, Italy and Spain would lay open before them and he would have the whole of Europe at his mercy. His one reverse at Vienna would be irrelevant; all past insults and reverses would be irrelevant; as he would ultimately be master of the world. At the end of the Divan Suliman made a declaration: "Those sons of dogs, whom I have already conquered and who were spared only by my clemency at Rhodes forty-two years ago, I say now that for their continual raids and insults they shall finally be crushed and destroyed!"

An illustration of Ottoman troops, including cavalry, elite Janissaries and other infantry, landing from transport ships during the Turkish invasion of Cyprus. An apparently unmanned galley is in the foreground of this picture from the *Súleymanname* made for Sultan Selim. (Ms. Haz. 3595, f.102b, Topkapi Lib., Istanbul)

14

OPPOSING COMMANDERS

THE MUSLIMS

Although Suliman did not accompany the expedition, his figure loomed large over the Muslim army. It was his vision that had set the invasion on course and he had masterminded every aspect of the campaign.

Sultan of the Ottomans, Allah's Deputy on Earth, Lord of the Lords of this World, Possessor of Men's Necks, King of Believers and Unbelievers, King of Kings, Emperor of the East and West, Emperor of the Chakans of Great Authority, Prince and Lord of the Most Happy Constellation, Majestic Caesar, Seal of Victory, Refuge of all the People in the World, Shadow of the Almighty Dispensing Quiet in the Earth – these were the full titles Suliman the First had gained since he had succeeded his father as Sultan of Turkey in 1494 at the age of 26. He was probably one of the few men of his own, or any other, age to be capable of living up to such high-blown praise. He had completely reorganised the government and administration of the empire, where he was known as the Lawgiver. The rest of Europe called him Suliman the Magnificent.

Under his rule the Turks had had only one failure, at the gates of Vienna in 1529, but the empire had gained Aden, Algiers, Baghdad, Belgrade, Budapest, Nakhichevan, Rivan, Tabriz, Temesvar and Rhodes. At Rhodes, after a magnificent defence, the Order of St. John had agreed to honourable surrender and evacuation of the island. On seeing the 70-year-old Grand Master, Villiers de l'Isle Adam, Suliman had been moved to clemency, but in the 42 years since, the Knights had taken up residence on the island of Malta and were raiding Turkish ships and possessions. Suliman's advisors were urging him to action. Suliman was now himself 70 and looked back on his former leniency towards the Knights

Luxury goods were not just exotic animals. In this 16th-century woodcut the central figure is a military dealer selling European captives to a slave trader, for resale in Constantinople. (Anne S. K. Brown Military Collection, Brown University)

with regret. He therefore determined to mount an expedition that would wipe them from the face of the earth. However, Suliman decided not to command the expedition in person, and set about creating a command structure.

Mustapha Pasha was designated commander of the Sultan's Army and co-commander of the fleet. He was from a family descended from the standard bearer of the prophet Mahomet. As such he was an aristocrat and, not surprisingly, a religious fanatic. He was a veteran of the Persian Wars and the Hungarian campaign and a skilled soldier but even among his own people he was renowned for his violence and brutality, and he held a particular hatred for Christians. He looked upon the expected defeat of the Knights as the crowning achievement of his life. Mustapha Pasha was the same age as Suliman, and like the Sultan, had fought in the campaign at Rhodes; he thirsted to finish the job.

Admiral Piali could not have been more different to his co-commander. He was born a Christian and was found as an infant abandoned in a field outside Belgrade in 1530 by the besieging Turkish army. Suliman had taken a liking to the boy and had him brought up in his own harem. When he came of age, Piali served in the Imperial Navy, where he soon proved himself a talented and enthusiastic officer. He had been successful particularly in the battle of Djerba and in his joint raid on the Italian coast with the pirate Dragut in 1558, when he captured thousands of slaves and much loot. Cementing his position in the royal family was his marriage to Suliman's grand daughter, making him the son-in-law of the heir to the throne.

The Sultan had ordered that Piali "reverence Mustapha as a father" and that Mustapha "look upon Piali as a beloved son".

There were two 'assistant' commanders appointed for the campaign, the Governor of Alexandria, El Louck Ali, who was a Turk and a skilled sea captain, and El Louck Ali Fartax. The latter was for a time the most active pirate in the Aegean Sea. He was also a renegade Christian and a former Dominican brother.

Torghoud, or Dragut Rais, as he was more popularly known, was the most famous pirate of his age, a skilled commander on both land and sea. His had been one of the voices urging the Sultan to attack Malta, and he had personal reasons for doing so. He had seen the Knight La Valette when the latter had been a galley slave after his capture by the Turkish captain Kurst Aly, and had secured some small privileges for him. Eight years later, when La Valette had escaped the oars, the tables were turned. Dragut had been defeated by the Genoese admiral Giannettino Doria, La Valette was on board the ship that had picked Dragut up and he had remarked to the pirate: "Monsieur Dragut, it is the custom of war," to which Dragut dryly replied: "And change of fortune".

Born in Anatolia in 1485 Dragut was of peasant stock, but one day the

Turkish pasha and two noblemen

governor of the region had happened to be passing through the village and had been impressed by his intelligence. The governor took Dragut to Egypt with him and had him educated, after which Dragut served in the Mamelukes as a gunner, where he became most skilled. Later he went to sea, which is where fortunes were to be made. Here also he came to the attention of a valuable patron, the famous Barbarossa. Starting as a gunner, he eventually acquired his own ship sailing out of Alexandria, and he soon attracted such a following that on Barbarossa's death in 1545 Dragut was his natural successor. The Turks called him 'The Drawn Sword of Islam', but his Christian foes were even more lavish in their praise. According to Admiral Jurien de la Graviere of France: "Dragut was superior to Barbarossa. A living chart of the Mediterranean, he combined science with audacity. There was not a creek unknown to him, not a channel that he had not sailed. Ingenious in devising ways and means, when all around him despaired, he excelled above all in escaping by unexpected methods from situations of great peril. An incomparable pilot, he had no equal in sea warfare except the Chevalier Romegas. On land he was skilful enough to be compared with the finest generals of Charles V and Philip II. He had known the hardship of captivity and he showed himself humane to his own captives. Under every aspect he was a character. No one was more worthy than he to bear the title of King."

Dragut also knew Malta well: he had raided it on seven occasions between 1540 and 1565. He had captured galleys of the Order, outwitted the great Admiral Andrea Doria, and led the raid that had captured Tripoli from the Knights in 1551. In the past he had had occasion to quarrel with the Sultan, but now that was all forgotten. Dragut was confirmed as Imperial Governor of Tripoli and Admiral of the Grand Porte with a gold-mounted sword and a jewel-encrusted copy of the Koran sent by Suliman.

Suliman had decided not to accompany the expedition. For this reason Dragut was given a watching brief over the co-commanders, who had been told to respect Dragut in all things and to accept his suggestions and advice.

THE CHRISTIANS

The structure of the Order of St. John and its sovereignty over Malta admitted of only one commander, and the fact that the Muslims never completely managed to cut off communications between the various strongholds on the island ensured that the entire blame for defeat or glory of triumph would belong to only one man – the Grand Master of the Order.

Jean Parisot de la Valette was born in 1494 in Provence into an old family descended from the original hereditary Counts of Toulouse. Among his ancestors were Crusaders who had followed France's Saint King Louis and several who had joined the Order of St. John of Jerusalem or 'The Holy Religion', as it was known. At the age of 20 he decided on this course himself, but unlike most of his ancestors – and most Knights – he was totally dedicated to the Order and lived by his vows. From the time he joined, he never again saw his family home or even his native land.

The dress of the Pasha was the typical attire of senior Turkish officers at the time and was not as impractical as it may at first appear. The robes of silk afforded some protection while keeping the wearer cool (in Italy during the Renascence there was some experimentation with 'silk armour', and it was found that multiple layers would stop certain sword cuts) and the extravagantly thick turban made quite an effective helmet. (Costumes of All Nations, 1907)

Jean Parisot
de la Valette,
Grand Master of the
Order of St. John of Jerusalem,
of Rhodes and of Malta. Even in
this engraving the calm determi-
nation and iron will are evident.
On his cuirass is engraved the
eight-pointed cross of the Order,
which symbolises the eight beat-
itudes but is today known to one
and all as the 'Maltese Cross'.
(Private collection)

Eight years after his investiture he was present at the Order's greatest disaster, the loss of the Island of Rhodes, which had been the Order's home since the loss of the Holy Land. On Rhodes, the Order had transformed itself from the classical idea of the Knight on horseback to a naval force. From their well-fortified and lush base they raided Turkish trade routes. La Valette soon proved himself as a naval commander and gained his own galley.

At this time he was described as "very handsome, tall, calm, unemotional, speaking several languages fluently – Italian, Spanish, Greek and Arabic". Turkish he learned by a less than conventional method: in 1541 he led his galley, the *San Giovani*, into action against the pirate Abd-ur-Rahman Kust Aly. For the only time in his life he was defeated. Badly wounded, he spent the following year as a Turkish galley slave. He was chained stark naked to a bench with five others and could expect to row for between ten and 20 hours at a stretch without a break, with only bread soaked in wine as sustenance – thrust into the mouth of anyone who looked likely to faint. If a slave did collapse, he would be flogged until he appeared dead and then thrown over-board. It was during this time that La Valette met Dragut for the first time. He finally gained his freedom in a prisoner exchange. As might be expected, anyone who survived this life was practically indestructible; if nothing else, La Valette was a survivor.

In 1554 La Valette was chief admiral of the Order's galleys, and he again met Kurst Aly on the high seas. This time La Valette was the victor, and he sent his captive, along with 21 other Turks, to the galleys.

La Valette's rise within the Order, if not meteoric, was steady. In his time he held every important post in the Order – Governor of Tripoli, Bailiff of Lango, Grand Commander and Grand Prior of St. Gilles, Lieutenant of the Grand Master and General of the Fleet. It was said of him that he was capable of "converting a Protestant or governing a king-dom", so when the Grand Master La Sangle died, in 1557, La Valette was unanimously elected Grand Master, even though he had not yet become a Knight Grand Cross of the Order.

Luckily La Valette had always thought that the Turks would lay siege to the island of Malta and he began to prepare for the possibility. Not that his predecessors had been idle in the 27 years that the Order had controlled the island: Fort St. Elmo had been built in 1552 to protect the harbour mouth. However, it was La Valette who ordered the construction of outer works that would enable it to withstand a siege.

La Valette also ran a spy system which was so efficient that by the autumn of 1564 he knew for certain that an attack was on the way. He was thus able to send out a call for the Knights of the Order throughout Europe to come to Malta, and to alert Don Garcea de Toledo, Viceroy of Sicily, to the plans of the Sultan.

THE OPPOSING ARMIES

THE MUSLIMS

The forces of Suliman the Magnificent were impressive indeed. The view of the Turks as a somewhat luxurious languid people which had developed during the downfall of the Ottoman Empire when Turkey was considered 'The sick man of Europe' had long since changed. The forces of the Sultan were by turns hated and feared by the common folk of the West, and respected for their fighting prowess by the military.

The elite of the troops were, unusually for the time, infantry. The Janissaries were probably originally formed as a bodyguard by the first sultan, Murad, about 1363, and was the backbone of an army that consisted almost exclusively of horsemen. By the manner of their formation they confirmed to the Christian West the barbarity of the Turk. The Sultan levied a draft or national service requirement on the Christian subjects of his empire, but this service was undertaken by children and continued for life. The boys were converted to Islam and under the tutelage of the most devout of Imams became fanatical soldiers of Mohammed. However, it is important to remember that the Janissaries

BOTTOM LEFT **Turkish cavalry officer, lancer and archer with lance and shield. (Costumes of All Nations, 1907)**

RIGHT **An arquebusier with two infantrymen, both with bows, and an officer of the Janissary corps. (Costumes of All Nations, 1907)**

Soldiers

Soldiers (janissaries)

ABOVE **Turkish infantry archer with an officer and standard bearer. (Costumes of All Nations, 1907)**

This illustration of the great battle of the Mohacs, in which the Ottoman army defeated the Hungarians, was painted in 1558 and comes from the magnificent _Súleymanname_ manuscript. It shows Janissary musketeers in the sort of uniforms – and with the same weaponry they used during their less successful attack on Malta. The plumes worn by their officers would not, however, have been used in combat. (Ms. Haz. 1517, f.220a, Topkapi Lib., Istanbul)

occupied an enviable position within Turkish society. The members of this corps had the opportunity to rise to high office not only in the army but in the empire at large. Their lot must have been envied by many in Christian Europe. This system was to go through so many permutations that the full story of the corps' origin remains shrouded in mystery, but certainly they were among the first troops to adopt firearms as their principal weapon. By the mid 16th century they made up about a quarter of the Turkish army; about 6,300 of them formed the elite of the invasion force.

The Iayalars, irregular infantry armed mainly with swords, numbered about 3,900 in the invasion force. They were religious fanatics who would take hashish before battle and, under the direction of the Imams, perform a Berserker-like charge heedless of casualties.

The main body of the force were the Spahis, numbering about 9,000. They had been drawn from Anatolia, Karamina and Romania. They were known chiefly for their cavalry, which at one time had made up the bulk of the Sultan's army. In siege operations cavalry is of limited use, but some did accompany the force. However, the bulk of the soldiers were armed with bows, crossbows and matchlocks.

The rest of the force was made up of 6,000 levies similarly armed, but the armada was accompanied by a fairly large number of renegades to both Christianity and Judaism, mainly from Greece and the Levant.

The Turks were extremely skilled in artillery and were fine engineers. Although there is no exact record of the number of guns transported to Malta it is recorded that 80,000 rounds of shot and 15,000 quintals of powder were brought over. Some of the guns were massive, and some were made with consummate skill to screw together once unpacked from the ship's hold. It should be remembered that, even with this vast inventory, they were planning for a siege which would last a few days at best, a few weeks at worst.

The entire Turkish force was dressed for warfare in the East, flowing robes of cloth and silk that would keep the wearer cool, very little armour (usually of leather), with helmets and shields of metal for the lighter armed troops. The vast turbans worn by the officers and some of the men were just as effective as metal against most sword cuts.

With the sailors and support troops sent to the island, the invasion force numbered no fewer than 40,000 men.

THE CHRISTIANS

The core of the defenders' force was still the armoured Knight, members of the Order of St. John. In many ways they were the Christian counterparts of the Muslim Janissaries – proud, brave, unswervingly loyal and members of an Order which was under the protection of the Pope,

though not under his jurisdiction. They were members of a 'religion', as it was termed, a religious Order with full vows of poverty, chastity, and obedience, but also trained as some of the finest fighting men of the day.

The Knights may have become sailors more than landsmen over the years but that had not meant a change in their outward appearance. They still wore the full field armour that they would have worn for combat on land. The main reason for this was that naval warfare of the time chiefly consisted of closing with the enemy until one could grapple his ship and then fight in the usual way, man to man.

Armour had reached its apogee at the beginning of the Renascence period; with its clean lines and sometimes boxy shape, it offered magnificent protection and only weighed about 100 pounds. However, the drawback of armour was the heat caused by the padded undergarments worn underneath, particularly in summer in a place like Malta. Indeed, in 1551 Sir John Upton, head of the English 'Langue', (Knights who spoke the same Langue, or tongue, served together) dropped dead of a heart attack while leading an attack on Dragut's men who were raiding the island, though it was said that he was a "large and corpulent man".

The armourer's art had also begun to atrophy: the optimum design for protection had been reached, and the only advances were in decoration, gilding and the rather elaborate and somewhat silly 'parade' armours favoured by the Italians, usually in pseudo-classical style. Although firearms had become common on the battlefield, they were not so effective that armour could be discarded to any great extent for the next 100 years. Some of the Knights had equipped themselves with 'Maximilian' armour, named after the German emperor who had had the first suit of this style made. It was much lighter than the usual harness, being made of plates that gained their strength from being heavily fluted, so that any blow was deflected away from the body of the wearer.

During the siege a scratch force was given the name of the Langue of England. Even though the only English Knight present was Sir Oliver Starkey, it was to preserve the memory of one of the most famous branches of the Order destroyed by Henry VIII. At the beginning of the siege 700 Knights were present to defend Malta.

Of the Order but not in the Order were the sergeants who, while not of a social standing to become full members, served as junior officers in the military structure and who in battle would hardly be distinguishable from the Knights. Even at this time, as the musket was beginning to gain ascendancy on the field, armour enabled these men to expose themselves to action that would otherwise have been fatal. The rest of the Christian force, the men-at-arms, consisted of native Maltese, with a few mercenaries and soldiers of fortune thrown in for good measure. Altogether the force numbered only about 8,500.

Although all the traditional weapons were used during the siege – sword, mace, pike and halberd – the musket was becoming the ordinary soldier's weapon. Although more expensive than the more traditional armaments, it required no particular skill or practice to master it. If an archer was killed, years of practice and skill were lost to the army, but if a musketeer went down, almost anyone could pick up the weapon and continue the fight. The musket used by the Christians was shorter than the Turkish one and though easier to load was not as accurate – as those who had to run the gauntlet of Turkish snipers found out.

In addition to the these troops, once the invasion began every able-bodied man, woman and child on the island must have taken part. Hardened by years of having to fend off Muslim raids (not always successfully), they were no strangers to fighting for survival, and their skill as swimmers helped the Order of St. John keep open lines of communication that would otherwise have been cut.

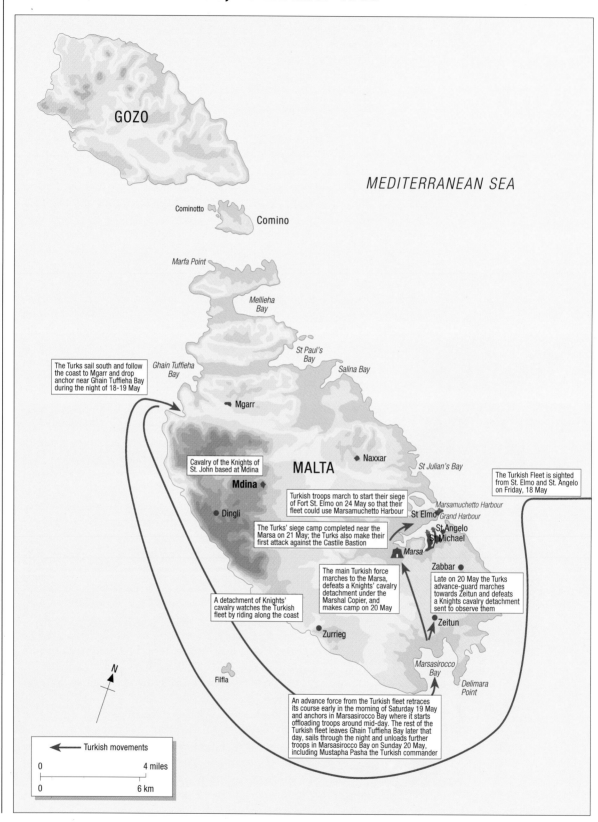

GOZO

MEDITERRANEAN SEA

Cominotto

Comino

Marfa Point

Mellieha Bay

Ghain Tuffieha Bay

The Turks sail south and follow the coast to Mgarr and drop anchor near Ghain Tuffieha Bay during the night of 18-19 May

St Paul's Bay

Salina Bay

Mgarr

Cavalry of the Knights of St. John based at Mdina

Naxxar

MALTA

St Julian's Bay

Mdina

The Turkish Fleet is sighted from St. Elmo and St. Angelo on Friday, 18 May

Turkish troops march to start their siege of Fort St. Elmo on 24 May so that their fleet could use Marsamuchetto Harbour

Marsamuchetto Harbour

Dingli

St Elmo *Grand Harbour*

St Angelo

The Turks' siege camp completed near the Marsa on 21 May; the Turks also make their first attack against the Castile Bastion

St Michael

Marsa

The main Turkish force marches to the Marsa, defeats a Knights' cavalry detachment under the Marshal Copier, and makes camp on 20 May

Zabbar

Late on 20 May the Turks advance-guard marches towards Zeitun and defeats a Knights cavalry detachment sent to observe them

A detachment of Knights' cavalry watches the Turkish fleet by riding along the coast

Zeitun

Zurrieg

Marsasirocco Bay

Delimara Point

N

Filfla

An advance force from the Turkish fleet retraces its course early in the morning of Saturday 19 May and anchors in Marsasirocco Bay where it starts offloading troops around mid-day. The rest of the Turkish fleet leaves Ghain Tuffieha Bay later that day, sails through the night and unloads further troops in Marsasirocco Bay on Sunday 20 May, including Mustapha Pasha the Turkish commander

Turkish movements

0		4 miles
0		6 km

THE CRESCENT ON THE HORIZON

The Chevalier Romegas was out on patrol with four galleys. He had been given orders that morning by the Grand Master in person. The lookouts at forts St. Elmo and St. Angelo had both reported ships on the horizon and his instructions were to assess the size of the attacking fleet but under no circumstances to engage them. Great sailor as he was, and much as he might have liked to cut out a few stragglers, this would have been extremely foolhardy. The enemy fleet consisted of over 200 vessels and the loss of even one Knight at this stage would have been of great importance, let alone four galleys.

The great armada sailed south. It was naturally assumed that they were heading for Marasirocco, with its excellent anchorage, but they sailed on up the west coast and finally dropped anchor at the bay near the village of Mgarr in the north-west. Members of the Order's cavalry, who had been tracking the fleet by land, galloped back to the Grand Master with the news. La Valette sent an immediate message to Sicily by a fast boat – "The Siege has begun. The Turkish fleet numbers about 200 vessels. We await your help." As he was soon to find out, the old adage is very true: the Lord helps those who help themselves.

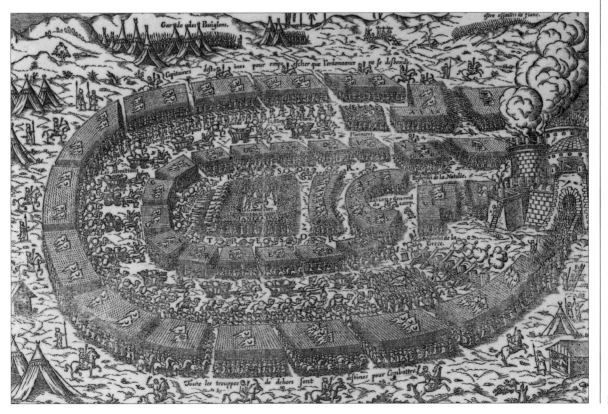

The help of the Lord arrived sooner than anyone expected. At this time, when every hour was of the greatest value to the Knights, the Turks showed indecision. Obviously decidng the anchorage they had chosen was a bad one, they again put out to sea and retraced their course to Marasirocco, the 'South Wind Harbour'. Unknown to the Turks, they had made an excellent choice, as it was only open to the south wind, which only rarely blew in summer and so would have served them for the whole campaign. However, this indecision over anchorage was to re-occur and cost them dear.

It took several days for the Turks to disembark. The Knights monitored their progress, and some initial skirmishes took place between the Knights' scouts and the Turkish foraging parties. As at Rhodes, no effort was made to prevent the landing or to engage the Turks; the Knights were outnumbered to such an extent that this was not an option. Instead, the Knights were going to adopt the same tactics as the ones they had used on Rhodes, to retire to the fortifications and then let the attackers spend their energy and numbers against the defence works. In this the island itself would aid them: although the fortifications were not as good as at Rhodes, there was not just one target for the Turks to concentrate on, so they would have to either distribute their troops between the various forts or concentrate on one and leave the others relatively unmolested. Furthermore, the island was not the lush and fertile Rhodes, and it was made even more inhospitable by the fact that the Knights poisoned the wells that lay outside their control as the Turks advanced.

The Order had four fortifications: Mdina, the old capital of the island; fort St. Elmo on Mount Sciberas, overlooking the sea; Fort St. Angelo, on the peninsula of Birgu; and on the next peninsula to it (Senglia), Fort St. Michel. Only the last two were mutually supportive, being on adjacent peninsulas only half a mile apart. However, St. Elmo guarded the entrance to Grand Harbour, into which the peninsulas projected. Mdina looked far more impressive than it actually was. In spite of the impressive appearance of the defences, they were old and crumbling, and it was undermanned and could not be re-supplied. This post was used as the base for the Order's cavalry. Not only was it the base from which raids could be mounted on the Turks, but since the cavalry was the only method by which the Grand Master could communicate with his various forces and even with the outside world, it was also at the very heart of the Order's command structure. The Mdina region was also one of the most fertile areas on the island. However, in the first of many missed opportunities the Turks decided to start elsewhere.

During various raids that the Knights had undertaken against the Turks, one of their number, Adrien de la Riviere of the Langue of France, had been captured. Under interrogation he refused to speak and was duly tortured. Eventually he cracked and cried out that the Post of Castille on the Birgu peninsula was the 'weak spot of the fort' and that its attack would bring Mustapha a quick victory. However, the post was one of the most exposed on the island and was therefore particularly well reinforced and manned.

This unusual print, which shows the back of the uniform of a Turkish lancer, was executed in the 18th century. However, the previous 200 years had seen almost no alteration in the dress of the Turkish soldier.

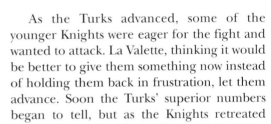

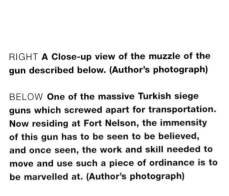

RIGHT **A Close-up view of the muzzle of the gun described below. (Author's photograph)**

BELOW **One of the massive Turkish siege guns which screwed apart for transportation. Now residing at Fort Nelson, the immensity of this gun has to be seen to be believed, and once seen, the work and skill needed to move and use such a piece of ordinance is to be marvelled at. (Author's photograph)**

As the Turks advanced, some of the younger Knights were eager for the fight and wanted to attack. La Valette, thinking it would be better to give them something now instead of holding them back in frustration, let them advance. Soon the Turks' superior numbers began to tell, but as the Knights retreated under the guns of the fort, Mustapha realised he had been tricked. The Christians had lost 21 dead and 150 wounded to about 300 Muslim dead in front of the walls and one captured standard, which now hangs in the conventual church. One Knight also took a bracelet from a Turkish officer he had killed. It was inscribed 'I do not come to Malta for wealth or honour, but to save my soul'. As has been stated since, all men who go to war think God is on their side.

As soon as Mustapha returned to camp he had de la Riviere bastinadoed to death. In this type of torture, the victim is beaten with thin rods until he dies of internal haemorrhage. The Knight had been perfectly aware of what his fate would be when he gave the false information. Both La Valette and Mustapha knew the calibre of their opponents: this was a fight to the finish.

Mustapha's next battle was with Piali, admiral of the Turkish fleet. In a heated council meeting Mustapha planned to capture Mdina, occupy the north of the island and then move on to Senglia and Birgu while part of the fleet blockaded Grand Harbour to prevent the arrival of reinforcements. He was overruled by Piali, who was now convinced that the fleet must be moved from Marasirocco to what he considered the safer anchorage of Marsamuschetto, the entrance to which, like Grand Harbour, was guarded by Fort St. Elmo.

THE ATTACK ON ST. ELMO

After the initial assault, the Grand Master had assumed, not unreasonably, that the attacks on Birgu and Senglia would be renewed, but two Christian renegades – men who had changed sides and religions in order to save their skins – decided to go over to the Knights. One of them had been a member of Mustapha's bodyguard and had been present at the stormy council meeting at which Mustapha's clever strategy had taken second place to Piali's concern for the Sultan's fleet. The renegades also told the Grand Master that the Turks did not think St. Elmo's capture would be very difficult, since it was a fort and did not have the reserves in the towns behind as did the other defence works. La Valette could not have chosen a better move for the Turks himself. He would begin strengthening St. Elmo immediately, and the longer it held out the more time he would have to work on the defences of St. Michel and St. Angelo, both of which the Turks would have to take in order to secure the island.

16th-century artillery in action, in a print after von Senftenberg. Musketeers in the centre of the formation protect the guns, which are firing grapeshot, while the mortars to the rear lob shells over the formation.

News was sent immediately to St. Elmo's bailiff, Luigi Broglia. He would have the honour of receiving the first assault. Chevalier Pierre de Massuez, who had recently arrived with 400 men from Messina, was sent with his command to join the defenders, along with 64 Knights who had requested the honour of serving in the defence of the fort. They were immediately rowed across the harbour to join the garrison and bring it up to a strength of about 600. The Grand Master had seen them off with the words "St. Elmo is the key to Malta".

The design of St. Elmo was well described by the Turkish engineers. "It is a star fort. There are four main salients, and the front, which we shall have to storm, is broken into bastioned form. The cavalier which rises to seaward is separated by a ditch. There is also a small ravelin. Both these outworks are connected to the main fort, the one by a drawbridge and the other by a fixed bridge."

The greatest drawback to the assault was to be the ground over which the Turks had to fight. Mount Sciberas, which overlooks the point and was the perfect site for the guns, was solid rock, thus offering no chance to dig entrenchments or even afford the slightest cover to the attackers.

Mustapha gave orders for the siege guns to be moved into position. These were so heavy and the roads so bad for the four and a half miles of the haul that even the cattle brought over as food were used to drag them into position. He also had the troops bring up baskets of earth from the lower ground to construct defences, and until these were complete he kept his men on the reverse slope to protect them.

The Turks were masters of siege warfare and the guns they brought with them were truly astounding. They included ten 80-pounders, two 60-pounders and an enormous 160-pounder Basilisk. Of course, the very nature of the weight of shot meant that these weapons had a slow rate of fire, but the weight of shot against fortifications was truly awesome. However, keeping the troops on the reverse slopes until the defences were constructed meant that the Knights were able to re-supply St. Elmo with impunity. On 24 May the bombardment began.

Back at St. Angelo a gun position was under construction to fire on the Turkish position on Sciberas, but other than that and the nightly infusion of volunteers, there was little that could be done except use well the time that was being bought. Within hours of the beginning of the bombardment the outer walls began to show signs of cracking, and snipers were picking off any of the fort's sentries who were unwise enough to stick their heads above the parapet. In fact the Turkish positions, covered by a camouflage of branches and leaves, gave St. Elmo's defenders no view of the snipers at all. With 40 years of experience the Turkish artillerymen were masters of their craft, and the relentless pounding of the walls by different weights and types of shot – now iron, now marble – always concentrated on the same spot was telling. By late May Mustapha had begun to site some of his guns to face St. Angelo, but he was being premature.

A galley of the Order of Malta under oars. This print shows well the graceful lines and elegant look of these 'greyhounds of the seas'. However, what cannot be conveyed is the smell that was the inevitable consequence of having the galley slaves chained to the oars. In use since classical times, this model of ship had just about reached the end of its useful life; in a very few years advances in naval technology would relegate the galley to history. (Private collection)

The assault and bombardment of Fort St. Elmo on 27 May 1565, as shown in a near contemporary Italian print. In the foreground the Turks are shown in considerable detail and with remarkably accurate costume, along with their tents. (Via Dr. David Chandler)

THE SIEGE BEGINS

On the day the siege of St. Elmo started La Valette had heard from the Viceroy of Messina, to whom a message had been sent when the Turks arrived. Instead of the help for which he hoped, the Viceroy vacillated, saying that it would take time to gather a large force and a small one would merely be slaughtered, to no effect. In other words, the Knights were on their own for the foreseeable future. It was therefore even more critical that every fort be defended to the last, and it was with something less than pleasure that the Grand Master received a delegation from the besieged St. Elmo. A group of Knights had slipped away to tell him of the position they were in. They said that trench work was encircling the fort, that the outer walls were crumbling and that the position was doomed. He listened in icy silence and then calmly remarked that they were relieved and need not go back to their post. Since he knew that it must be held, he and a specially selected force would go to St. Elmo to replace the Knights. Shame got the better of their terror, and all the Knights begged to go back to what they, and everyone else, knew was certain death. None the less, there were volunteers to go to St. Elmo every night, in the relief boats that delivered fresh troops and brought the wounded back to Birgu.

The next day, when the guns opened fire on St. Elmo, the guns sited on St. Angelo joined them, and the bombardment interfered with the slight covering fire which was being put up from across the harbour; the

The bow-fired version of the incendiary device, of necessity somewhat smaller than the matchlock type, was nonetheless deadly.

Turkish engineers pushed their trenches inexorably closer, and Janissary snipers were moved closer to the fortifications. However, the dramas of the day were just beginning. Early in the day Admiral Piali was wounded by a shard of rock sent up by a Christian cannonball, and as he was nursing his wound in his tent an unexpected sea battle developed.

ST. AUBIN RUNS THE BLOCKADE

Chevalier St. Aubin, a Knight Commander of the Order and one of its finest naval commanders, had been on patrol off the African coast. He had been warned by the Grand Master that battle may already be joined by the time he returned, and was told to watch for the signs. Incredibly, instead of turning tail at the sight of the blockaded harbour, St. Aubin sailed straight for it, obviously attempting to run the blockade. For Piali this was the second wound of the day. He immediately sent out six of his galleys to deal with the madman. Nothing changed, however, and St. Aubin came on and began to engage the Turkish ships with his bow chaser. As he came closer, he must have realised the impossibility of breaking through the enemy fleet and so he disengaged from the action and turned towards the north. The Turks gave chase but could not keep up with the swift galley, and in the end only the ship of Mehemet Bey was in pursuit. This was St. Aubin's chance to show what a galley of the Order could do. He executed a classical tactic by having one bank of oars hold water while the other rowed at full speed, the galley turned in its own length and was now the attacker. Mehemet Bey turned tail and ran. St. Aubin turned and set his course for Sicily.

Piali was beside himself with rage. His fleet had been disgraced and humiliated by just a single Christian ship while the Christians and – what to Piali was worse – his fellow Turks looked on. Mehemet suffered public degradation from Piali, which ended with the ultimate insult of being spat at in the face.

In the early morning of 29 May musketry could be heard in the forward trenches of the Turks – Christian musketry. Colonel Mas and the Chevalier Medran had silently lowered the drawbridge during the night and had led out a sortie. As the dawn broke, the Grand Master and the council had a new panorama before them: not only had the engineers working in the trench fallen back, but the advance guard of the Turkish army was also in full retreat. Mustapha knew what to do only too well. He emerged from his tent with the cry of "Janissaries, forward!" and forward they came, in vast numbers, sweeping all before them and driving the sortie back beyond the trench works. When the smoke and dust cleared, the white-robed Janissaries and the crescent standards were to be seen on the outer works of the fort, overlooking the inner walls of St. Elmo.

The matchlock used to fire an incendiary device. The container, possibly made of thin pottery and filled with Greek Fire, would shatter on impact, scattering its contents on its target. This device would be of most use against wooden or indeed any flammable defence works, but it could also be a very useful anti-personnel weapon.

THE ARRIVAL OF DRAGUT

The next day the members of the Order both at St. Elmo and St. Angelo were brought to the battlements by a curious manoeuvre of the Turkish fleet. Each ship in turn sailed close to the shore, fired its guns at St. Elmo and then rejoined the fleet. It was a useless exercise: those cannon balls that hit the fort did little damage and the rest either bounced off the cliff or sailed completely over the fort, sometimes hitting their own army on the other side. At least one vessel ran aground. Then it was realised that this was no serious attack but a ceremonial one – the Turkish equivalent of a 21-gun salute. To add to the troubles of the Knights, Dragut had arrived.

Although never acknowledged as such, by the Sultan's instructions and his own reputation Dragut was de facto commander-in-chief. The ex-pirate, ex-galley slave turned governor was not pleased with what he found. He was of the opinion that Mustapha's original plan should have been followed, securing the north of the island first and leaving St. Elmo until last, when it would have fallen like a ripe apple. Now, though, they were committed to the siege and it must go on or honour would be lost. He saw at once that the reason St. Elmo was holding out was because of the nightly re-supply from St. Angelo. He re-sited guns to try to stop this and ordered some of the guns to be taken off the fleet to help properly enfilade the fort. However, Piali, as usual, would not hear of anything of the kind until his ships were in the harbour, so the shortage of guns continued and the re-supply of the fort was only affected by Turkish patrol boats in the harbour. Dragut's last instruction was that all the fort's outworks must be taken – certainly a job for the Janissaries. He then left to set up his camp among the trenches. At 80, he was still very much a fighting soldier, and much as he liked his comfort in peacetime, he wanted no part of a silk-lined tent in war. With a feeling of foreboding, the Knights watched as new gun emplacements took shape on Gallows Point and Tigne which would soon add to the fire enfilading the fort. The fire began on 3 June, St. Elmo's Day. Until then, however, the Order's cavalry had sallied out from Mdina, attacking the Turkish base camp, supply trains and gun teams, and even putting one of Dragut's new batteries out of action; nothing in itself of great concern, but a constant drain on enemy resources and an annoyance to their high command.

Just before dawn on 6 June some Turkish engineers were reconnoitring near the ravelins of St. Elmo. Seeing no movement, they crept closer, and to their astonishment they found all the guards asleep. They silently slipped away. Quite why no sentry was on duty at this critical time of day, when attacks can be expected, is not certain – perhaps exhaustion,

This print, of a spectacular firework display held as part of victory celebrations, shows various incendiary devices of the period, including trumps, rockets, firework hoops and Greek Fire. (Moeurs, *Usages et Costumes au Moyen Age*, 1871)

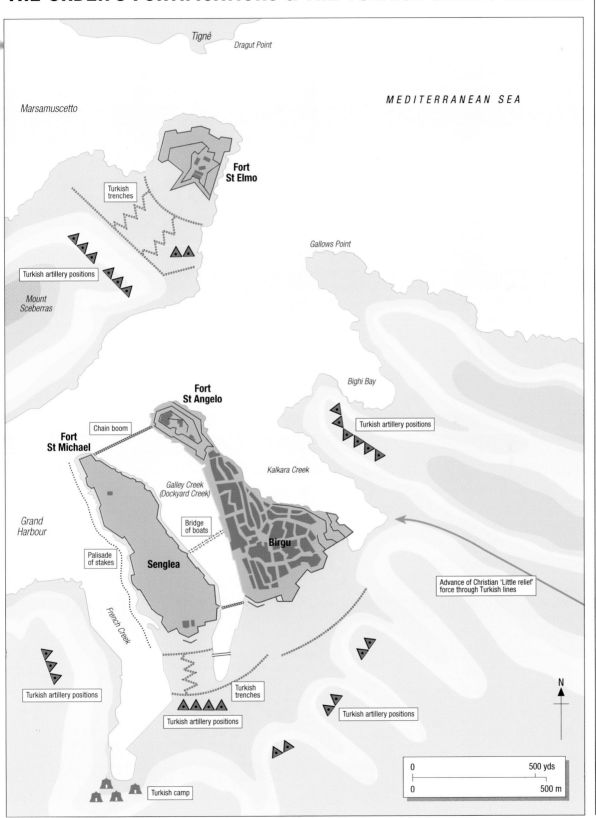

Tigné

Dragut Point

MEDITERRANEAN SEA

Marsamuscetto

Fort
St Elmo

Turkish
trenches

Turkish artillery positions

Mount
Sceberras

Gallows Point

Bighi Bay

Turkish artillery positions

Fort
St Angelo

Chain boom

Fort
St Michael

Kalkara Creek

Galley Creek
(Dockyard Creek)

Grand
Harbour

Bridge
of boats

Birgu

Palisade
of stakes

Senglea

Advance of Christian 'Little relief'
force through Turkish lines

French Creek

Turkish artillery positions

Turkish
trenches

Turkish artillery positions

Turkish artillery positions

N

Turkish camp

0	500 yds
0	500 m

perhaps he had been killed while his comrades slept and no-one had noticed. It was an opportunity that would not present itself again, and the Turks were not going to miss it.

The Janissaries were formed by Dragut and Mustapha and silently advanced carrying scaling ladders. They made no noise until they were at the top of the ladders. Then an Imam shouted: "Lions of Islam! Now let the sword of the Lord separate their souls from their bodies, their trunks from their heads! Liberate spirit from matter!" and the white robed elite rushed down on the position. A plank bridge connected the ravelin to the fort, and over this a few survivors ran while an artillery piece over the portcullis kept the Turks at bay while it was raised to allow the survivors in. When the Janissaries re-grouped, they rushed right up to the portcullis and fired through it. Now was the time to use weapons that the defenders had prepared for just such a moment: Greek Fire, a sort of napalm molotov cocktail in thin earthenware pots that could be thrown up to 30 yards; the Trump, a primitive flame thrower which gave off a flame several yards long fed by sulphur resin and linseed oil; and the firework hoop made of light wood soaked in brandy and oil then wrapped in wool which was repeatedly soaked and dried in similar flammable liquids and impregnated with gunpowder. This last weapon was specifically designed as an anti-personnel weapon against the Turks. When lit they were then thrown over the walls using tongs, and would land on or in front of the attackers, several of whom could be entangled in one hoop. Their traditional Turkish robes would soon catch fire and the effect was devastating.

Because of these weapons, particularly the hoops, Mustapha eventually called off the attack. Even with 2,000 Turkish casualties, all from the elite of the Janissaries, against just 10 Knights and 70 soldiers it was no time for rejoicing. The Turks could well afford the men to gain such an advantage. Even before the attack was called off the emplacements were being worked on by Turkish engineers and more guns were being brought up. As if to remind the defenders of their fate, when they went to chapel that evening to give thanks, they found one of their confreres, a Knight who had been mortally wounded that day, had dragged himself there and was lying dead before the altar.

The next day the Turks tried again. Cannon boomed incessantly, and with their new positions the Turks commanded the whole of the fort's courtyard, so that anyone venturing into the open would be shot. During the initial bombardment whole sections of wall collapsed, and in places so little was left that it could not be manned. It was therefore with some surprise that when the Janissaries again ran forward to the attack they met with withering fire and all the rest – Trumps, Greek Fire and hoops. This, and the only partly filled-in ditch, made the attack falter and finally fail. As the Turks left their blazing screaming colleagues to their fate, the most intense bombardment yet opened on the fort and some thought the final hour had come.

A mullah preaching to Muslims in the minbar of a mosque. In some ways the Muslim idea of 'Jihad', or 'Holy War', had a lot in common with the Christian Crusade, though their belief in 'the will of Allah' was in some ways to work against the Muslims in the latter stages of the siege. (Historical Military Productions, New Orleans)

TOP **A long bronze 16-pounder gun cast specifically for the Knights of Malta. Though dating from 50 years after the battle, this piece gives a good idea of the type of armament with which the Knights resisted the Turkish invasion. (Author's photograph)**

ABOVE **The muzzle of the 16-pounder above. The gun was removed from Malta when the island was under British protection and is now on display at Fort Nelson.**

TO EVACUATE ST. ELMO?

That night the commanders of St. Elmo came to the conclusion that the fort was no longer defensible. They sent the Chevalier de Medran, a senior and well-respected confrere, to the council to explain the position. De Medran was not of the stamp of the earlier delegation; he had been in the fight from the beginning and his views were given a hearing. He left that night and immediately met with the council. De Medran explained that the fort was indefensible and that any defenders left were sure to die. This would deny their services to the next fortification to be attacked yet not prevent the loss of St. Elmo. If a stand were to be attempted, further reinforcements would be needed which would be an active drain on the valuable garrisons of Senglia and Birgu. His recommendation, therefore, was to evacuate the garrison and blow up the remnants of the fort.

Some of the council agreed with the assessment but the Grand Master did not. He now revealed for the first time the full text of the message from Don Garcea de Toledo, Viceroy of Sicily, that he was preparing a relief force and would be able to come to their aid by 20 June, but that he would not risk his fleet if St. Elmo had fallen. La Valette continued: "We swore obedience when we joined the Order. We swore on the vows of chivalry that our lives would be sacrificed for the faith whenever, and wherever, the call might come. Our brethren in St. Elmo must now accept that sacrifice." He knew that he must hold out for the chance of relief, but even if it did not come, the only way that the Order stood any chance of driving off its foes was to hold every position to the last and let their attackers know it. De Medran knew it was a death sentence, as did the 15 Knights and 50 soldiers from the Mdina garrison who volunteered to go back to St. Elmo with him. However, on his return, some of the younger Knights were not best pleased with their fate. They did not consider sitting in a ruined fort waiting for the end their true lot in life. They begged to be permitted to sally out of the fort and meet death in an attack on the Turks. The Grand Master replied to the messenger: "The laws of honour cannot necessarily be satisfied by throwing away one's life when it seems convenient. A soldier's duty is to obey." However, he did appoint a commission of three Knights from three different Langues to make a further report for him.

While at St. Elmo two of the commissioners were of the opinion that the fort could hold out a few days more, a third was less than discreet. The Chevalier Castriota declared that all that was needed were fresh men and a fresh approach and the place could be held indefinitely. A near riot broke out at this remark, and order was only restored when the alarm sounded, not because the Turks were actually attacking but to calm the hotheads. On his return to Birgu, Castriota repeated his remarks to the Grand Master, who gave him permission to raise a volunteer force to garrison St. Elmo under his command. In a short while he raised 600 men to follow him. La Valette wrote to the rebellious Knights at St. Elmo: "A volunteer force has been raised... Your petition to leave is now granted... Return... to the Convent... where you will be in more security... I shall feel more confident when I know that the fort... is held by men whom I can trust implicitly."

Within minutes of the letter being read, no-one would have dreamed of leaving his post; indeed, a swimmer was sent back, begging the Grand Master not to relieve them. Only 15 Knights and 100 soldiers were sent as reinforcements.

Dragut was becoming frustrated. In spite of their successes his troops had not taken the fort, and a raid by the Order's cavalry had knocked out his battery on Gallows point, relieving the pressure on the boats re-supplying St. Elmo. He re-established the position using some of his heaviest guns which could be used against the harbour wall of St. Elmo, while commanding the harbour approaches between St. Angelo and St. Elmo, and which could later be traversed to attack St. Angelo. Mustapha had determined to try a surprise night attack against the fort on 10 June and so a bombardment was kept up all day long. As night fell and the defenders might have expected the bombardment to cease, the attack came.

The Turks too had incendiary weapons. Added to those of the Knights, the blaze seemed to turn night into day. Wave after wave of Turks crashed against the walls and were driven back with cannon, pike, sword and fire. The Turks' anti-personnel weapons were not as effective

THE MORTAL WOUNDING OF DRAGUT

Dragut and the other leaders of the Turkish invasion force led from the front and were willing to expose themselves to enemy fire when necessary. The magnificent uniforms of these Turkish leaders and their staff also made them a highly visible target. It was while supervising the construction of new artillery emplacements overlooking Grand Harbour that Dragut was struck down by a splinter of rock thrown up by a cannon-ball. He was followed shortly after by the Aga of the Janissary Corps. Dragut lived a few more days but died the day the Fortress of St. Elmo fell. With him the Turks lost their most capable leader and perhaps the finest naval commander in the Mediterranean.

as those of the Knights, since St. Elmo's defenders were wearing armour rather than silk and had set up great barrels of water near the walls. When the sticky burning goo landed on them, they plunged into the water and extinguished the flames, the Turks had no such provision so they roasted alive. By the end of the attack the Turks had lost 1,500 men to the Knights' 60.

The reason that there was no fear of death in the Turks was their absolute belief in the words of their Mullahs as they called them to prayer and urged them to battle. All who died in Holy War would go to paradise, where they would spend an eternal afternoon under the shade of the palm trees, refreshed by wine (forbidden to them in this life) and clear water and welcomed by divinely beautiful houris, in whose arms a climax would last ten thousand years. With such promises ringing in their ears, what soldier would not exchange the discomforts of a campaign, even through a time of agony, to enjoy such delights?

This fanaticism was put to use by Mustapha on 16 June. Rather than send in Janissaries as the first wave, he decided to hold them in reserve and send the Iayalar fanatics in first followed by the dervishes. Finally the Janissaries, eager to avenge the death of their commander a few days before, were unleashed. Mustapha and Dragut stood side by side in full view on top of a ravelin during the attack, the latter re-directing fire to the sections of wall that were not under attack by his infantry. However, he could not stop enfilading fire from the south wall or the balls fired from St. Angelo that were ripping into the Turks. After another 1,000 casualties the Turks retreated, but the Christians had lost many of their leaders and the battery on Gallows point would soon cut them off for good.

Earlier that day, the Turks had had a worrying situation of their own. Two Christian galleys had been spotted off the north of the island. Some of the reinforcements being gathered on Sicily, growing frustrated at the Viceroy's tardiness, had decided to try a landing. After holding position for most of the day, they realised that it would be suicide to do so and retired. Admiral Piali was again beside himself. To him this was yet another example of how vulnerable the fleet would be until he could get them into the harbour, particularly since his galleys had once more been unable to catch the swifter Christian craft. However, he deployed the fleet to cover the possibility of any hit and run raid, and urged Mustapha to get on with it.

DRAGUT IS WOUNDED

The next conference of the Turkish commanders saw Dragut once more emphasising that the garrison of St. Elmo must be absolutely cut off from all supplies and that the concealed battery on its southern corner, which had done so much damage, must at all costs be destroyed. To this end he proposed to extend the earth and brushwood

The breech of the gun described on page 36, showing details of the decoration. Below the figure of John the Baptist are the arms of the Order (left) and of the Grand Master (right). (Author's photograph)

A Turkish ship (sails not shown) which illustrates the armaments and fields of fire of a vessel of the Turkish fleet. Note how the shot leaving the bow chaser is depicted, indicating the use of Greek Fire. (Anne S. K. Brown Military Collection, Brown University)

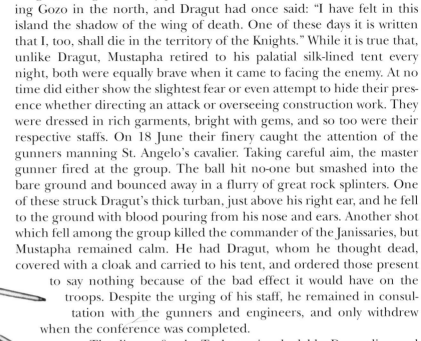

screen down the eastern flank of Mount Sciberas to the edge of Grand Harbour. This work he and Mustapha would oversee in person. For Dragut, the fight was very personal. His brother had been killed attacking Gozo in the north, and Dragut had once said: "I have felt in this island the shadow of the wing of death. One of these days it is written that I, too, shall die in the territory of the Knights." While it is true that, unlike Dragut, Mustapha retired to his palatial silk-lined tent every night, both were equally brave when it came to facing the enemy. At no time did either show the slightest fear or even attempt to hide their presence whether directing an attack or overseeing construction work. They were dressed in rich garments, bright with gems, and so too were their respective staffs. On 18 June their finery caught the attention of the gunners manning St. Angelo's cavalier. Taking careful aim, the master gunner fired at the group. The ball hit no-one but smashed into the bare ground and bounced away in a flurry of great rock splinters. One of these struck Dragut's thick turban, just above his right ear, and he fell to the ground with blood pouring from his nose and ears. Another shot which fell among the group killed the commander of the Janissaries, but Mustapha remained calm. He had Dragut, whom he thought dead, covered with a cloak and carried to his tent, and ordered those present to say nothing because of the bad effect it would have on the troops. Despite the urging of his staff, he remained in consultation with the gunners and engineers, and only withdrew when the conference was completed.

The disaster for the Turks was incalculable: Dragut lingered on for a few days, but was never again able to help in any of the planning. He was the recognised commander, the only one who could co-ordinate the army and navy successfully. He was the one man whose advice would be heeded by both Mustapha and Piali; literally and metaphorically, the Turkish forces had had their brains knocked out. That evening, a Turkish deserter crossed the lines and gave the Grand Master the news.

For the Turks, the next day was not much better. They had one piece of luck when a powder mill at St. Angelo caused a spark in a magazine, which blew up killing six men. The cheers of the Turks were stilled by a cannonade into their ranks. Rumours had begun to spread about the death of the aga and the wounding of Dragut, and while Mustapha was again in conference in view of the enemy, Chevalier Antonio Grugno, who commanded St. Elmo's cavalier, directed one of his cannon at the group. This time the Master General of the Ordnance was killed, Mustapha's second in command. Grugno was almost immediately picked off by a Turkish sniper and was ferried over to the hospital that night. After midnight de Miranda sent a message to the Grand Master that the loss of the fort could be expected at any hour, and the next evening he sent another

A 16th century infantry officer armed with sword and pike and wearing a cuirass and what appears to be a 'chapeau de fer', or iron hat, of civilian shape.
(*The Army Pageant*, 1900)

THE FALL OF ST. ELMO'S FORT

**The Turks finally took the fortress of St. Elmo.
On the other side the Knights' garrison was wiped
out, except for a handful of Maltese soldiers who
escaped by swimming across Grand Harbour.
During the collapse the defenders did have
time to burn the relics and regalia of their
church to prevent it falling into enemy
hands. Their commanding officers, De
Guras and De Medran, are said to have
been too weak to stand and so sat in
chairs during the final attempt to defend
the breach as the Turks swarmed through.**

which said: "Every new reinforcement sent into the fort is lost. It is cruelty therefore to send any more men to die here." Once more the Grand Master sent a mission over to St. Elmo to assess the situation. This time their boat was under fire all the way there and back, with men killed on both the outward and return journey: Dragut's battery and snipers were in place. The report that came back was that the fort was surrounded and that it might be able to withstand one more attack at most. Several members of the council suggested evacuation after such an eventuality, but the realists knew that that was an impossibility.

The date of 21 June is the feast of Corpus Christi, which the Knights celebrated every year; 1565 was no exception. Dressed in formal robes with the white cross of the Order, the Grand Master and all available Knights joined the clergy in solemn procession through the streets. On returning to the conventual church, they knelt in prayer for their confreres at St. Elmo. At almost the same time, Turkish troops had managed to advance unseen along the shore of Marsamuschetto to occupy the fort's outer defences. When the garrison began receiving musketry from the rear, they realised the cavalier had fallen. Immediately cannon were turned on the cavalier and the musketry ceased, but during the night Turkish snipers took out position there in such numbers that they could not be moved. The morning of 22 June heralded another bombardment and attack with the Turks now so close to the defenders that the guns of St. Angelo dared not fire for fear of hitting their confreres. There was more hand-to-hand fighting than before, and a group of Turks got onto the walls where they were engaged by the defenders. Suddenly the wall collapsed and the Janissaries made a rush for the breach.

The snipers opened fire and reinforcements began to arrive. The defenders were falling back. Chevalier Melchior de Montserrat, governor of St. Elmo now that Luigi Broglia was incapacitated, immediately brought a cannon to bear on the cavalier and the musketry ceased. Defenders rushed to the breach and the day was saved, though Montserrat was killed by a musket ball on the spot. For six hours the battle raged, until Mustapha sounded the recall. Another victory for the Knights, but this time they had lost 200 men and no replacements would be coming. In fact the Grand Master did try to send more volunteers, but the well-sited batteries and musketeers drove the five boats back.

Remarkably, among the volunteers that one would naturally expect, Knights, Christian soldiers and Maltese, there were two Jews; that men who almost certainly knew Christian persecution firsthand should volunteer for certain death with the Knights is nothing if not remarkable.

The moment of victory by the Turks in a Christian camp. An officer leads his men in the slaughter and capture of the defenders and looting of the camp. (Courtesy of the Anne S. K. Brown Military Collection, Brown University)

ST. ELMO FALLS

The garrison knew their final hour had come: the chaplains heard the confession of every man and said mass. Afterwards the church plate was buried under the stone floor of the chapel and all the wooden fittings and tapestries brought out and burned so that they would not be used as trophies or desecrated. Then they began the slow ringing of the bell.

Dawn on Saturday 23 June 1565 saw Piali's fleet heading towards the stricken St. Elmo. As they came within range they opened up with their bow chasers and then peeled off, making a dash for the waters of

The fate of captives not sold as slaves: victims are beheaded, used for target practice or impaled. In the centre of the picture one body is being flayed by a Turk, who seems to have brought along a skinning knife for the purpose. (Anne S. K. Brown Military Collection, Brown University)

Marsamuschetto. This signalled the mass Turkish assault. The Knights and soldiers were ready – as ready as they could be for this last battle – but the forces were overwhelming. The entire Turkish force was used – Janissaries, Spahis, Iayalars and Levies – all in one unstoppable rush. De Guras and De Miranda were too badly wounded to stand, so they had themselves placed in the breach, sitting in chairs. In the initial rush De Guras was knocked to the ground but managed to find his feet and fought with a pike before he was decapitated; Colonel Mas was literally torn to pieces; others were cut down at the door of the chapel in a last ditch effort to defend it from the Turks. As this went on, one of the Knights lit the signal fire that told Senglia and Birgu that St. Elmo had fallen. Nine Knights were taken prisoner – five Spaniards, three Italians and one Frenchman. They were never ransomed and never heard of again. Five Maltese soldiers saved themselves by jumping from the rocks and swimming to Birgu at the last moment; they were the only survivors.

The Turkish losses were horrendous – about 8,000 men, almost a quarter of their strength in the attack, against about 1,500 Christians, a ratio of one to six. There were sick and wounded by the thousand, for beside battle casualties there were those laid low with enteric fever, malaria and dysentery. The Turkish hospital was almost as big as the camp. Worst of all, Dragut was out of action.

The first thing Mustapha did after entering St. Elmo was to send a message to Dragut to tell him of the victory. Dragut raised his eyes to heaven and died. As he looked across the harbour at St. Angelo, Mustapha Pasha is said to have remarked: "Allah! If so small a son has cost us so dear, what price shall we have to pay for the father?"

The fall of St. Elmo on 23 June in one of a series of Italian prints. The artist has drawn a clear distinction between the senior Ottoman officers on the right, the elite Janissaries in the centre, and various other Turkish assault troops beyond the lines of artillery emplacements on the left. The Turkish banners are also based upon real examples, or at least upon sketches of real flags. (Via Dr. David Chandler)

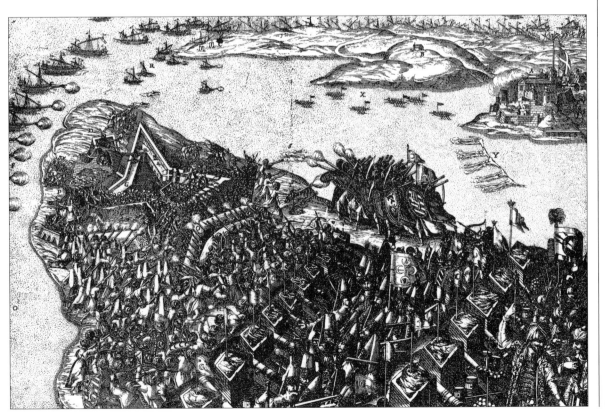

FORT ST. MICHAEL

La Valette was prepared for the onslaught that was to come. His main defensive positions were the two fortified spits of land that stuck out into Grand Harbour. On one (Sciberas) was built the fort of St. Michel, the walls of which completely surrounded the point, and on the other was the town of Birgu, which was heavily walled on the landward side and whose point was the site of fort St. Angelo. The two forts were joined by the Great Chain, a defence work that was exactly what its name suggests. The chain cut off the water between the two spits from outsiders but could be lowered to allow in friendly ships. Food supplies were good, according to one account: "As for food, they had seven or eight thousand bushels of wheat, not counting the barley which had been cut at the beginning of the harvest, and of which they had about three thousand bushels." In addition, they had good supplies of olive oil, cheese, butter, salted meat, sardines, tunny and dried cod. Water was no problem either, since they had 40,000 casks and an active spring in Birgu. La Valette ordered the destruction of all dogs in the town, with no exceptions, not even his own hunting pack, so they would not be a drain on the supplies. The one thing the Order did not have was reinforcements. Despite his promise to come by 20 June if St. Elmo had not fallen, there was no sign of the Viceroy's relief force.

It was the eve of the feast of St. John, and although gunpowder could not be spared, the Knights lit celebratory bonfires in honour of the saint. As the Turks clearing St. Elmo looked across the harbour, they were dismayed: even after the fall of their fort the Knights were celebrating the feast of their patron saint in their usual way. They needed something to think about.

BODIES IN THE SEA

On the morning of 24 June St. Angelo's defenders rose to see the heads of their confreres who had died defending St. Elmo looking at them from across the water and in the water an even grizzlier sight. The decapitated bodies had been stripped and nailed to wooden crosses that were being brought ashore by the morning tide. The Grand Master went down to view them for himself, accompanied by his Latin secretary, Sir Oliver Starkey, the only English knight at the siege. This was a clear declaration by Mustapha: war to the finish, no quarter asked or given. In those days it was usual to ransom prisoners; obviously this was not to be countenanced on Malta.

Cavalry officer armed with a matchlock pistol. The officers of the landing force would have presented an appearance very similar to this. (Grosses' Military Antiquities, 1778)

A later print of the city of Valetta (built after the siege), which shows all the salient points of the engagements. The tip of the promontory facing the viewer is the site of St. Elmo; to the right, Marsamuschetto, which Piali insisted on having as his harbour; to the left, Grand Harbour, with the promontories of Birgu and Senglia extending into it.

La Valette knew what he must do. He must accept the challenge and let his enemy know that he was not intimidated. What followed is perhaps the most criticised aspect of the siege, but only by those who look at it from the comfort of an armchair at the remove of over 400 years. La Valette ordered his cannon to fire on the Turks, but when the shot landed, they found that it was not made of iron or stone, it was the heads of all of the Knights' Turkish prisoners who had just been executed.

La Valette then addressed his council: "What could a true Knight more ardently desire than to die in arms? And what could be more fitting for a member of the Order of St. John, than to lay down his life in the defence of his faith? We should not be dismayed because the Muslim has at last succeeded in planting his accursed standard on the ruined battlements of St. Elmo. Our brothers – who have died for us – have taught him a lesson which must strike dismay throughout his whole army. If poor, weak, insignificant St. Elmo was able to withstand his most powerful efforts for upwards of a month, how can he expect to succeed against the stronger and more numerous garrison at Birgu? With us must be the victory." Then he addressed the soldiers, men-at-arms and towns-people: "We are all soldiers of Our Lord, like you my brothers. And if by ill chance you lose us and all your officers, I am quite sure that you will not fight with any less resolution."

REINFORCEMENTS GET THROUGH

Certainly resolution was necessary: even now the guns on mount Sciberas were being transported back down or re-sited to command St. Angelo and St. Michel, and engineers were surveying their future trench works. While making his own preparations for the coming attack La Valette received some good news. A small relief force had arrived on the north of the island on the very day St. Elmo fell. Under pressure from members of the Order, the Viceroy had sent two of his galleys to accompany two of the Order's ships to try to break through under the command of the Chevalier de Robles. Don Juan de Cardona, the naval commander, was specifically ordered not to land if St. Elmo had fallen. However, the scout he sent out to ascertain the situation only reported back to Robles, who decided to try to slip through the lines to Birgu at night. De Cardona did not find out the truth until all the troops were ashore and it was too late. De Robles' force consisted of 42 Knights, 20 gentlemen volunteers from Italy, three from Germany, two from England and 600 imperial Spanish infantry from the garrisons of the Two Sicilies.

The arrival of a small group of Christian reinforcements during the night of 5 July 1565, from a near contemporary Italian print. The Cross banner of the Hospitaller Knights of St. John, along with what appears to be the banner of the Spanish Crusading Order of Santiago, is shown centre.

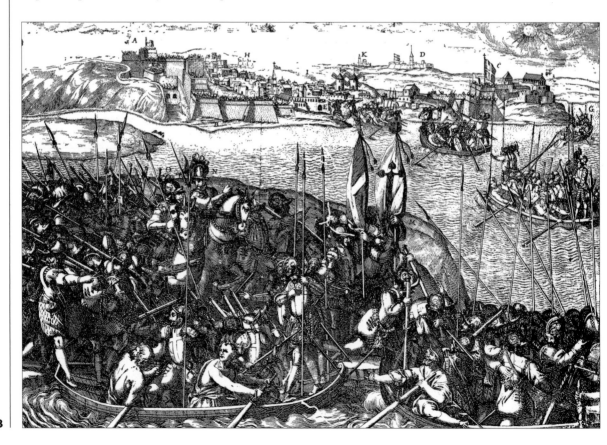

As soon as they were landed they began a march down the west coast of the island and De Cardona put off to sea, with the galleys still unaware of St. Elmo's fall. Skirting the Turkish camp and avoiding their patrols, they circled well south of the camp and round the trench lines that were being constructed, sending messengers on ahead to tell the garrison of their arrival. They came down to the harbour where the village of Kalkara stands today to the shore of Kalkara Creek. The relief force had been particularly lucky: a mist, almost unknown at that time of year, had covered them like a thick fog. They avoided all patrols and when they reached the shore, boats were waiting to ferry them to Birgu. The Turks had boats in the harbour too, but no-one spotted them.

Pike men armed with pike and sword were considered the elite of the infantry regiment. They provided the 'hedge' from which the musketeers could emerge to fire and withdraw into for protection. (Grosses' Military Antiquities, 1778)

The relief force reached the town without losing a single man and the garrison was ecstatic. Next morning, to wild cheering, their banners were placed on the wall where the Turks could plainly see them.

For the first time Mustapha flinched. Less than a week ago he had wanted to kill every Christian on Malta. Now he looked at the task ahead of him and the state of his army and decided that he would offer La Valette the same terms that Suliman had offered the Knights at Rhodes (terms that the then Grand Master had accepted): honourable surrender, the garrison to march out under arms and with banners flying, to take ship and unmolested be allowed to depart for Sicily.

Fearing that a Turk would not return alive from the fort, Mustapha chose an old Christian slave from his household to deliver the message. The old man was led blindfold through the city until he stood before La Valette, who now showed himself the complete master of diplomacy and psychology. He listened impassively, and when the message was delivered, answered with two words: "Hang him." The old man fell to his knees and begged for his life, which is what La Valette wanted. Ordering his eyes bandaged again, he was taken to the gate which led to the bastions of Provence and Auvergne. Then the blindfold was removed so that he could see the ditch sinking below him and the walls towering above and he was asked for his opinion. "The Turks will never take this place," he replied. Then La Valette spoke: "Tell your master that this is the only territory that I will give him. There lies the land that he may have for his own – provided only that he fills it with the bodies of his Janissaries." He was then shown serried ranks of Knights and men-at-arms and some of the most impressive cannon. In complete abject terror he soiled his

The musketeers were fast becoming the backbone of all infantry regiments and in siege warfare they were certainly the most effective one. In just over 100 years the musket would dominate the battlefield. (Grosses' Military Antiquities, 1778)

breaches, and after being blindfolded again he was returned to the Turkish lines.

Mustapha thought he had been more than generous with his terms – perhaps too generous. That his envoy should have been treated in such a way and sent back with such a message sent him into a fury. He vowed to kill every member of the Order. The fleet was now safe, and the only consideration was the reduction of the fortresses. Preparations continued with renewed vigour. On the Corradino Heights, looking across French Creek to St. Michel, he set up a battery to provide crossfire with those sited on Sciberas. In another quite brilliant stroke (or perhaps a tactic copied from the now dead Dragut, since Dragut had used the tactic before), he dismantled some of the boats and had them carried overland to the Marsa, where they were put in the water to attack the forts of the Knights from their own harbour. As the Grand Master and council watched, they considered what this would mean: they could not pass St. Angelo's guns to attack Birgu from the north, they could not enter Dockyard creek because of the chain defence so the attack would be on Senglia from the south.

As they were pondering this, a Knight looking across the harbour to the shore of Sciberas saw a Turkish officer waving at him. Immediately he got a boat and some men and started across the water to pick him up. As they approached they saw that a party of Turks had also seen the officer and were running towards him so fast that they would surely cut him off. As they closed on him, the officer flung himself into the water although it soon became evident that he was unable to swim. Immediately three men from the boat dived overboard to rescue him. He was brought before the Grand Master for appraisal. This man, it turned out, was no ordinary Turkish deserter but a Greek aristocrat captured as a young man. His family, the Lascaris, were descended from the emperors of Byzantium. Although he had successfully risen to high rank with the Turks, the heroic defence of the Knights had reminded him that he was baptised a Christian and was fighting with the very barbarians who had driven the princes of his family into exile. He freely and happily told the council all the plans that he

50

was privy to and then enthusiastically fought in the defence. He confirmed La Valette's appraisal of the situation but was able to reveal the full plan. The main attack would fall on St. Michel, but troops would be landed all along the peninsula. Already as the guns were being sited on the Corradino heights the snipers were in position to harass the sentries and workers, so preparations would have to be carried out at night.

The plan was simple but brilliant. La Valette ordered the building of a palisade, actually in the water, along the whole south of the Senglia shoreline. The stakes were driven into the sea bed and linked together with chain which passed through iron hoops that encircled the tops. In a few places the sand was not firm enough or the water too deep to fix the stakes, so here masts and spars were linked together to complete the defence. Even working only at night the defence was completed in nine days.

As an extra safeguard, a similar palisade was constructed on the north side of Birgu, stretching from the fort of St. Angelo in front of the posts of Castile, Germany and England. Naturally there were few actual English members of the Order. Since its dissolution in England by Henry VIII, all the English Knights had either renounced their vows or left the country, and it was in recognition of past services to the Order that the Grand Master had designated one of the posts England. The command of that post was given to the only English Knight present, Sir Oliver Starkey who, as the Master's Latin secretary, acted not unlike a chief of staff. However, now he had with him the two English soldiers of fortune who had been forced to leave England as Catholics and had come to Malta with the relief force. Their names are recorded as John Smith and Edward Stanley.

Before attacking, Mustapha attempted to destroy these defences. First he sent over swimmers with axes to assault it, but they were driven off. One was killed and several others injured by the Maltese soldiers, who were far better swimmers. Later Mustapha sent out boats with ropes which were fastened to the chain and then brought back to shore, where capstans were set up. This time he did succeed in pulling up some stakes, but once again the swimmers went out, cut the hawsers and repaired the damage. This failure, however, did not delay the attack.

Some days earlier Mustapha had been joined by reinforcements of his own. Hassem, Viceroy of Algiers, son-in-law of Dragut, had arrived with troops. He toured St. Elmo with Mustapha and rather arrogantly said that he could not understand how it had managed to hold out for so long. Perhaps, he opined, the attacks were not pressed with sufficient vigour. In support of his views he asked that he and his Algerians be permitted to lead the coming attack. His second-in-command, Candelissa, would command the seaborne attack and he himself the land. Probably with an inward smirk at the rashness of youth, Mustapha consented.

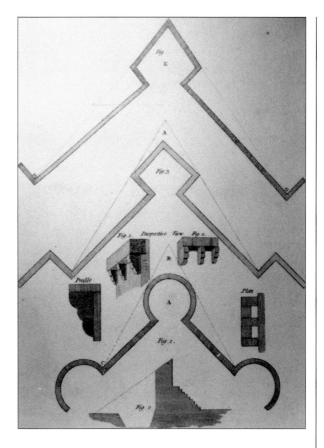

The principal of successive lines of defence. If one or even both of the outer defensive walls are taken, there is still an inner defence with a ditch sloping upwards, from which to fire upon the attackers, and an overhanging lip from which hot oil Greek Fire or other missiles might be hurled down. (Grosses' Military Antiquities, 1778)

Typical dress for a cavalry officer of the period: three quarters armour with leather boots, and armed with sword and pistol. (Grosses' Military Antiquities, 1778)

THE TURKS RESUME THE ATTACK

On the morning of 15 July the boats were loaded for their trip across the Marsa and up Grand Harbour. Mustapha ordered the attack to begin. In the lead were three boats carrying the Imams, who proclaimed Holy War to the faithful and doubtless recounted their vision of paradise for those about to die. Following were the bejewelled officer corps of the Turks and Algerians, and then, according to one eye-witness, innumerable small boats, "a sight truly most beautiful – if it had not been so dangerous".

The oarsmen pulled hard but the workmen had done their job well and the boats were stopped dead by the palisade and chain, within musket range of the defenders. Though deadly, the fire was not supported, for some reason, by two mortars which had been mounted for that purpose on the walls. Candelissa drew his scimitar, ordered his men forward and plunged into the water. His men followed, as soon as they were in shallow enough water to wade. They held their shields over their heads against the bullets and Greek Fire that was hurled against them. In spite of the great numbers that fell, they pressed on and began to scale the walls.

The landing of the amphibious troops was the signal for Hassem to attack by land. He and his men no doubt felt they had to make good his boast about "attacking vigorously". Cannon smashed shot and shell into them, but the great holes torn in their ranks did not stop the onslaught. Without waiting for the wall to be breached, they came on with ladders and scaled the walls, to be met by the Knights in hand-to-hand combat. Occasionally the struggling groups would lose their footing and tumble into the ditch.

Suddenly there was a tremendous explosion near the tip of Senglia. A powder magazine had blown up, taking a section of the wall with it, making a breach and driving back the defenders. Chevalier Zanoguerra, the commander of the post, led a counter-attack which began to drive the Muslims back. His heroic actions inspired those around him, but when he was shot dead the counter-attack faltered. When La Valette saw the Turkish standards in the breach, he immediately ordered reinforcements across the bridge of boats built for this contingency. The new troops inspired those already engaged, and the crisis in that section passed. This was not the only contingency that the Grand Master had made as Mustapha Pasha was to find out.

From Mustapha's point of view, and indeed that of any other observers, the point of crisis had come and he had a coup de gras prepared. He had a reserve of ten boats, packed with 100 Janissaries each, which he now sent to attack the point of Senglia. With all the defenders engaged on the south and west walls, they would land above the chain defence in Dockyard Creek, assault the north and tip the balance. From St. Angelo another pair of eyes was on the boats, those of the Chevalier de Guiral. The post that he occupied was in an interesting position – he commanded a battery that had so far not fired a shot. It was situated almost on the waterline of the fort and was specifically designed to protect the entrance to Dockyard Creek. This battery had gone completely unnoticed by the Turkish engineers and now 1,000 of Mustapha's crack troops were about to attempt a landing only 200 yards from the battery. De Guiral ordered his five guns loaded with bar, chain and grape shot. As the boats massed for landing their troops, the order to fire was given. Complete devastation was the result. The first salvo sank several of the boats and damaged the tenth. Bodies and debris were flung in all directions as the water erupted; further salvos finished the job. One boat managed to limp back to its base, but the other nine were sunk and 800 Turks were dead.

The fight continued with ferocity. In the blazing heat of midday even women and children manned the walls to fling Greek Fire and stones on the Algerians. In the end, after five hours the attack began to slacken and finally ended – but woe betide any Muslims still on Senglia. The Maltese – in no mood to take prisoners – cried: "No quarter! Remember St. Elmo!" Even Candelissa barely escaped with his life. As the Turks and Algerians withdrew from St. Michel, the defenders opened the gate and pursued them, showing that, for all his experience in siege warfare, Hassem had never faced such an enemy.

The disastrous Ottoman assault upon Fort St. Michel on 15 July 1565 is illustrated in an near contemporary Italian print. This series of pictures was made for propoganda reasons to celebrate the great Christian victory over the infidel Turks. Not surprisingly the enormous Muslim casualties and the despair of their commanders in the foreground is given great prominence. (Via Dr. David Chandler)

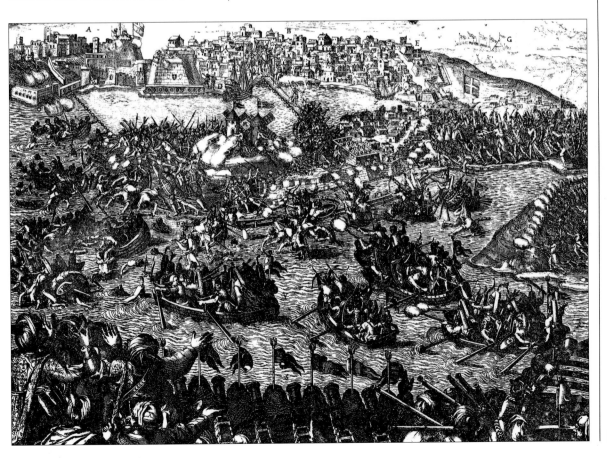

THE DESTRUCTION OF THE JANISSARIES' BOATS
Because the land walls of Senglia were so strong, Mustapha Pasha, commander of the Turkish army, attempted an amphibious landing across Grand Harbour. But the Turks did not know that the defenders had an artillery position concealed almost at water level in the Fortress of St. Angelo, designed to stop just such an attack. This was commanded by Chevalier de Guiral. Two salvoes were all that were needed to sink nine of the ten Janissary boats and those wounded men who struggled ashore at Senglia were slaughtered by the Maltese inhabitants – no prisoners were taken.

The furious Mustapha began a heavy cannonade from Corradino Heights and Mount Sciberas. If nothing else he would keep the garrison awake all night. Among the Christian dead were many famous Knights, in particular Frederick of Toledo, son of the Viceroy of Sicily. He had been left on Malta by his father as a guarantee that aid would be sent, and although he had been under the personal care of La Valette he had been unable to contain his enthusiasm during the attack. He had slipped across the bridge of boats unnoticed and was blown to bits on Senglia's ramparts, a fragment of his cuirass killing a companion. The total Christian losses for the day were 250; the Turks and Algerians lost about 3,000, their bodies thick around the walls and crusting the shoreline. That night many Maltese fished for bodies, as Napoleon's troops were to do in Egypt, to strip the gold ornaments and gems from the officers' uniforms and weapons. This harvest continued for many days.

CRISIS AND REPRIEVE

LEFT The principle of the siege tower. Made higher than the wall, the soldiers on the upper level try to keep the defenders pinned down while those on the next level down storm the walls via the drawbridge. The lower floors hold the reserves who will follow the first wave across the bridge and exploit any success. (Grosses' Military Antiquities, 1778)

BELOW Typical dress of a cavalry trooper or dragoon of the period: less heavily armoured than the officer, he carries a pair of pistols and a carbine, in addition to his sword. Body armour is restricted to a cuirass and a light helmet. (Grosses' Military Antiquities, 1778)

With the fatalistic view that it was the will of Allah and that all would be accomplished in His time, Mustapha prepared carefully for the next assault, Hassem had had his proud boasts discredited, but he had confirmed that the Knights intended to die rather than fall back one inch. Mustapha now planned to do on a larger scale what he had done to St. Elmo, completely surround and cut them off and then attack everywhere at once. What would be the use of a bridge by which reinforcements could be moved from one place to another if all the troops were engaged? True, both of the fortresses were stronger than St. Elmo, but Piali's fleet was patrolling the sea to make sure no more reinforcements got through and the arrival of De Robles' force had encouraged him to extend the sapping works down from Mount Salvator to Kalkara Creek, and Salvator itself he occupied with 16 guns, including two 300-pounders. Once this headland was occupied, the garrison would be cut off – or almost cut off.

What Mustapha never fully counted on was the commitment of the native Maltese to his destruction. Not only were they excellent swimmers, but they knew every nook and cranny of the land. At no time was the Grand Master unable to get a message through to Mdina and thence via small boat to Sicily. For a while Mustapha had hoped that the Maltese would revolt against their 'European masters'. They were, after all, of Arabic stock and they had a language that was so similar that they both referred to God as Allah. But when an approach was made to the population, he saw how useless it was to try to suborn their deep and abiding faith. His agents received the reply that they would rather "be the slaves of St. John than companions of the Grande Turke".

With Hassem taking no further part in the action, Mustapha put Piali in command of the force that was to attack Birgu, while Candelissa would command the fleet. He himself would command the attack on Senglia and Fort St. Michel. In preparation for the attack yet another battery was sited on the peninsula of Bighi, and from every side a constant cannonade rang out day and night on the defenders.

La Valette had not been idle all this time. He had anticipated a seaborne attack on Birgu and so sunk barges of stones along its Kalkara Creek shoreline and linked them together with chain, as had been done off Senglia. He also set gangs of slaves to building stone barriers across some of the streets of the town. The work was exposed, and many of the slaves were killed by the bullets of their co-religionists trying to prevent the building of further defences.

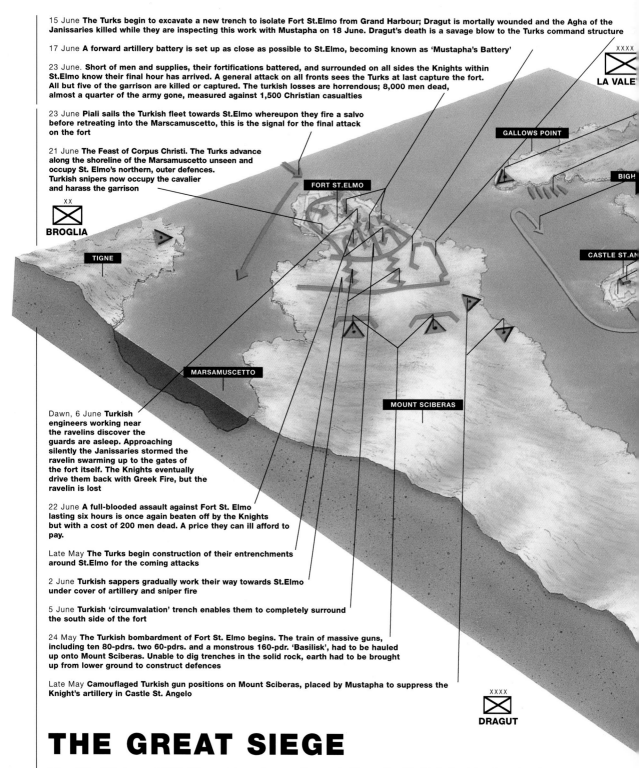

15 June **The Turks begin to excavate a new trench to isolate Fort St.Elmo from Grand Harbour; Dragut is mortally wounded and the Agha of the Janissaries killed while they are inspecting this work with Mustapha on 18 June. Dragut's death is a savage blow to the Turks command structure**

17 June **A forward artillery battery is set up as close as possible to St.Elmo, becoming known as 'Mustapha's Battery'**

23 June. **Short of men and supplies, their fortifications battered, and surrounded on all sides the Knights within St.Elmo know their final hour has arrived. A general attack on all fronts sees the Turks at last capture the fort. All but five of the garrison are killed or captured. The turkish losses are horrendous; 8,000 men dead, almost a quarter of the army gone, measured against 1,500 Christian casualties**

23 June **Piali sails the Turkish fleet towards St.Elmo whereupon they fire a salvo before retreating into the Marscamuscetto, this is the signal for the final attack on the fort**

21 June **The Feast of Corpus Christi. The Turks advance along the shoreline of the Marsamuscetto unseen and occupy St. Elmo's northern, outer defences. Turkish snipers now occupy the cavalier and harass the garrison**

XXXX
LA VALE

GALLOWS POINT

FORT ST.ELMO

BIGH

XX
BROGLIA

TIGNE

CASTLE ST.AN

MARSAMUSCETTO

MOUNT SCIBERAS

Dawn, 6 June **Turkish engineers working near the ravelins discover the guards are asleep. Approaching silently the Janissaries stormed the ravelin swarming up to the gates of the fort itself. The Knights eventually drive them back with Greek Fire, but the ravelin is lost**

22 June **A full-blooded assault against Fort St. Elmo lasting six hours is once again beaten off by the Knights but with a cost of 200 men dead. A price they can ill afford to pay.**

Late May **The Turks begin construction of their entrenchments around St.Elmo for the coming attacks**

2 June **Turkish sappers gradually work their way towards St.Elmo under cover of artillery and sniper fire**

5 June **Turkish 'circumvalation' trench enables them to completely surround the south side of the fort**

24 May **The Turkish bombardment of Fort St. Elmo begins. The train of massive guns, including ten 80-pdrs. two 60-pdrs. and a monstrous 160-pdr. 'Basilisk', had to be hauled up onto Mount Sciberas. Unable to dig trenches in the solid rock, earth had to be brought up from lower ground to construct defences**

Late May **Camouflaged Turkish gun positions on Mount Sciberas, placed by Mustapha to suppress the Knight's artillery in Castle St. Angelo**

XXXX
DRAGUT

THE GREAT SIEGE

May 19 - 23 June, 1565. Viewed from the north-west. Once the Turkish fleet had put ashore they set about besieging the Knights fortifications. The plan was to isolate and capture each fort one at a time, and entrenchments and artillery positions were prepared to knock out the first, St.Elmo. However, the Turkish plans would be soon set back as the siege became a long war of attrition, involving fierce fighting and heavy losses.

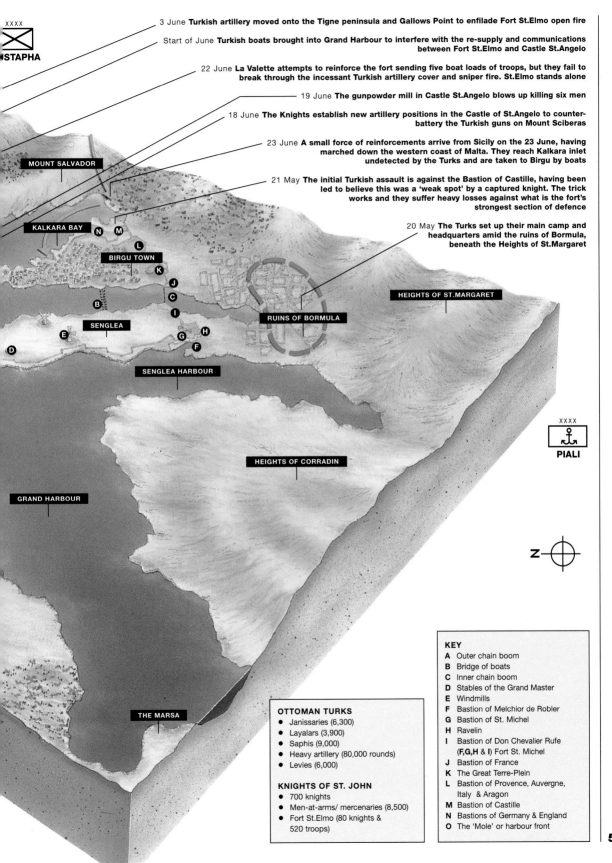

XXXX

STAPHA

3 June **Turkish artillery moved onto the Tigne peninsula and Gallows Point to enfilade Fort St.Elmo open fire**

Start of June **Turkish boats brought into Grand Harbour to interfere with the re-supply and communications between Fort St.Elmo and Castle St.Angelo**

22 June **La Valette attempts to reinforce the fort sending five boat loads of troops, but they fail to break through the incessant Turkish artillery cover and sniper fire. St.Elmo stands alone**

19 June **The gunpowder mill in Castle St.Angelo blows up killing six men**

18 June **The Knights establish new artillery positions in the Castle of St.Angelo to counter-battery the Turkish guns on Mount Sciberas**

23 June **A small force of reinforcements arrive from Sicily on the 23 June, having marched down the western coast of Malta. They reach Kalkara inlet undetected by the Turks and are taken to Birgu by boats**

21 May **The initial Turkish assault is against the Bastion of Castille, having been led to believe this was a 'weak spot' by a captured knight. The trick works and they suffer heavy losses against what is the fort's strongest section of defence**

20 May **The Turks set up their main camp and headquarters amid the ruins of Bormula, beneath the Heights of St.Margaret**

MOUNT SALVADOR

KALKARA BAY

N M

L

BIRGU TOWN

K

J

C

B

I

SENGLEA

E

G H

D

F

HEIGHTS OF ST.MARGARET

RUINS OF BORMULA

SENGLEA HARBOUR

HEIGHTS OF CORRADIN

XXXX

PIALI

GRAND HARBOUR

Z

THE MARSA

OTTOMAN TURKS
- Janissaries (6,300)
- Layalars (3,900)
- Saphis (9,000)
- Heavy artillery (80,000 rounds)
- Levies (6,000)

KNIGHTS OF ST. JOHN
- 700 knights
- Men-at-arms/ mercenaries (8,500)
- Fort St.Elmo (80 knights & 520 troops)

KEY
A Outer chain boom
B Bridge of boats
C Inner chain boom
D Stables of the Grand Master
E Windmills
F Bastion of Melchior de Robler
G Bastion of St. Michel
H Ravelin
I Bastion of Don Chevalier Rufe
   (**F,G,H** & **I**) Fort St. Michel
J Bastion of France
K The Great Terre-Plein
L Bastion of Provence, Auvergne, Italy & Aragon
M Bastion of Castille
N Bastions of Germany & England
O The 'Mole' or harbour front

As the first day of August drew to its close, La Valette may well have wondered what had happened to the relief force that was supposed to have reached him over a month before. They were now in high summer, with temperatures in the 90s every day, and although food, water and ammunition were not a problem, another all-out attack could not be long delayed. The very next morning was proof of that.

ALL-OUT ATTACK

As the first rays of sun fell upon the twin peninsulas of Senglia and Birgu so did the first projectile of the fiercest bombardment yet to shake the island. So fierce was the fire that it was heard 100 miles away. Every point of the defences came under fire, but St. Angelo itself came under crossfire from Mount Salvator, Gallows Point, Mount Sciberas and even the captured St. Elmo. St. Michel was likewise pounded until it was impossible to distinguish the stone walls from the stone dust that hung in the air. Then the Turks attacked from all sides, and continued attacking for six hours. Five concerted attacks where they actually gained small footholds were flung back with the savagery of those literally fighting for their lives, and when the attacks were finally called off the banners of the Order were still flying proudly from their forts.

For a further five days Mustapha continued the bombardment, and on the morning of 7 August, when the defenders could see nothing but Turkish troops surrounding them, they knew that another time of trial was looming. The guns ceased fire and the waves of enemy troops fell upon their objectives. As the troops attacking the Post of Castille came forward, they headed for a breach in the outer defences. The rubble from this breach had almost filled in the ditch and it must have looked like an ideal objective. As the defenders gave way and ran back, the Turks streamed after them only to find an inner wall barring their path. They had nowhere to go and could not retreat for the press of soldiers who were also making for the breach. Now the defenders opened fire on the Turks trapped between the two walls. Musketry, Greek Fire and firework hoops killed hundreds of them. As they wavered and began to flee, the defenders attacked and hacked down as many as they could. However, they retained their discipline and did not follow the Turks out of the defences; instead they immediately set about repairing the breach.

On Senglia, however, things were not going so well. The simultaneous attack had succeeded and St. Michel looked set to fall as the Turks pressed further and further into the fort. No men could be spared from Birgu to stabilise the situation. The 70-year-old Mustapha saw that his hour had come. He drew his sword and led his Janissaries to the attack, at the very moment that the attack on Birgu was being repulsed. If the Christians had needed a miracle to save them, they got one. Suddenly the Turkish trumpets sounded the recall. The Janissaries would only fall back when ordered to do so by their aga (general), and the ramparts that only moments ago were thronged with victorious Turks were silent. The reason for this was that Mustapha had got word that a large force of Christians were attacking the camp. The supposition was that a relief force had arrived after all. The only Christians on the island were the defenders, so it must be Don Garcea de Toledo and reinforcements, must it not?

THE TURKISH CAMP IS DESTROYED

All that had been possible for the garrison of Mdina had been to act as a staging post for the Grand Master's messages and send out the odd cavalry raiding party. That morning, however, the Governor of Mdina had heard the incredible bombardment and surmised that it could only be a major attack. Calculating that this would leave the Turkish camp only lightly guarded, he ordered the Chevalier de Lugny to take all the cavalry and destroy the camp. The march into position had taken some time, as they naturally wished to avoid any Turkish patrols. They had skirted the island until they were south-west of the Marsa then formed their ranks and charged. With only a few sentries the whole camp had been at their mercy. Tent ropes were cut and tents set on fire; the sick and wounded were massacred and as many of the horses as possible were captured; those that were not were killed or hamstrung.

This was the scene of devastation that greeted Mustapha on his return. For a while he did not understand: there was every evidence of a large force doing this but no army facing him, in fact no-one but his own dead and dying in sight at all. Suddenly he realised what had happened and how he had been cheated of victory at the very moment that it was in his grasp. So far he had lost over 10,000 men and only had the ruins of St. Elmo to show for it. "By the bones of my fathers I swear that when I take these citadels I will spare no man. All shall I put to the sword. Only their Grand Master will I take alive. Him alone I will lead in chains to kneel at the feet of the Sultan."

Several days later La Valette and Sir Oliver Starkey were pouring over the latest dispatch from Don Garcea de Toledo, which stated that before the month's end he would bring 16,000 troops to their aid. The Grand Master summed it up in a few words: "We can rely no more upon his promises". That evening he addressed the council and had his words

LA VALETTE LEADS THE COUNTER-ATTACK

One of the most desperate moments in the siege came after a Turkish mine destroyed part of one of the bastions defending the land wall of Birgu. The Turks almost immediately won a foothold on the main fortifications and began to enter the town itself. But La Valette, the Knights' commander, refused to allow a withdrawal and instead led a counter-attack. Inspired by his example, soldiers and townsfolk together drove back the Turks. During this bitter struggle La Valette was wounded in the leg, but he still refused to leave the fight until the enemy's flags had been thrown down from the wall.

recorded so that they could be distributed among the defenders. "I will tell you now, openly, my brethren, that there is no hope to be looked for except in the succour of Almighty God, the only true help. He who has up to now looked after us will not forsake us, nor will he deliver us into the hands of the enemies of the Holy Faith. My brothers we are all servants of Our Lord, and I know well that if I and all those in command should fall, you will still fight on for liberty, for the honour of our Order, and for our Holy Church. We are soldiers and we shall die fighting. And if, by any evil chance, the enemy should prevail we can expect no better treatment than our brethren who were in St. Elmo. Let no man think that there can be any question of receiving honourable treatment, or of escaping with his life. If we are beaten we shall all be killed. It would be better to die in battle than terribly and ignominiously at the hands of a conqueror."

As that message was sent out, another went with it. Pope Pius IV had promulgated a bull which granted a plenary indulgence to any of the faithful who died fighting the Muslims in that they would have died for their faith. By this act, any sin debt would be wiped out and they were assured of reception into glory. This affected every man, woman and child on the island, for no-one was safe and all did their part, even in just supplying the fighting men or throwing rocks at the advancing Turks. La Valette sent another message to the Viceroy, not because he expected him to do anything but because he hoped the members of the Order who were in Sicily would make their own way to Malta if they could. He told of the hardships, the overflowing hospitals and the ruined defences,

Unlike most of the other pictures in this series of Italian 16th-century prints, the Ottoman attack upon the Post or Bastion of Castile on 21 August 1565 is illustrated in relative close-up. The Knights and their men on the right maintain a steady fire as the Turks make their assault over the ruined walls from left, supported by artillery on the far left. The Christian commander, La Valette, directs the defence at the centre of the picture. His coat-of-arms, quartered with those of the Order of Hospitallers, is prominently shown on the shield carried by a small figure by his right leg. (Via Dr. David Chandler)

and ended with: "It would not be right for one particular section of the Order to be spared when the whole body is exposed to almost inevitable loss."

POINT COUNTERPOINT

In fact deep discussions were in progress in Sicily. The Viceroy argued that Malta was lost and, sad as that might be, he could not waste the lives of the emperor's troops in a fruitless attempt to save an island that did not now even belong to him, while no other monarch in Europe had sent aid. Far better that the soldiers should be held back for a possible attack in Europe if one should come. The alternative view was of course that if the Turks were to take Malta, then an attack on Europe would be almost inevitable. With such a magnificent harbour, the fleets of Suliman would dominate the Mediterranean and the next island for conquest would probably be Sicily and southern Italy. But apart from that argument, the island had been Philip II's gift under feudal law, and the Knights had always acknowledged their feudal obligations. Was His Most Catholic Majesty going to abandon them because they were being attacked by enemies of the faith? Don Garcea seemed finally to realise his predicament and his responsibility, but time was fast running out.

A print showing the use of the petard. The idea was to place the explosive device as close to the wall or door as possible and direct all the force in the desired direction. The fact that this device often went wrong, with dire results to the operator, gave rise to the expression 'hoist by his own petard'. (Private collection)

UPS AND DOWNS

For the first time Mustapha was attempting conventional siege warfare. He was constructing siege towers and had begun mining operations. Such methods had not been possible before, particularly mining which had been precluded at St. Elmo by its being built on solid rock. However, here it was possible, and again a concerted attack was planned, this time against a single point, the Spanish Post of Castille. A tower would be built higher than the walls and meanwhile the post would be undermined. In those days a mine was just that – a shaft hand-dug by labourers and held up with timbers. It would be extended under the enemy fortification and then on cue the timbers would be collapsed. The ground would cave in and, if the work had been done well, so would the wall on top.

The Egyptian engineers toiled for days in the humid darkness while the defenders above strained to hear what was going on. Even with a constant bombardment it was possible to hear some activity below, the soil being only about six feet deep and set on sand and limestone. The mine had to be dug under the ditch and the explosives placed under the wall. Mustapha had decided to try using the Knights' own strategies against them; he would attack Senglia in force and wait for reinforcements to be sent from the Post of Castille over the bridge of boats, then explode the

THE GREAT SIEGE

24 June - 15 July, 1565. Viewed from the north-west. After St.Elmo had been taken the Turks now turned their attention to the final capture of the fort itself. For this they would have to attack on all fronts to stretch the Knights resources until an eventual weak point was exploited. Mustapha was now reinforced with fresh troops under the commnad of the Viceroy of Algiers Hassem and proceeded with his planned attacks which he knew must succeed soon.

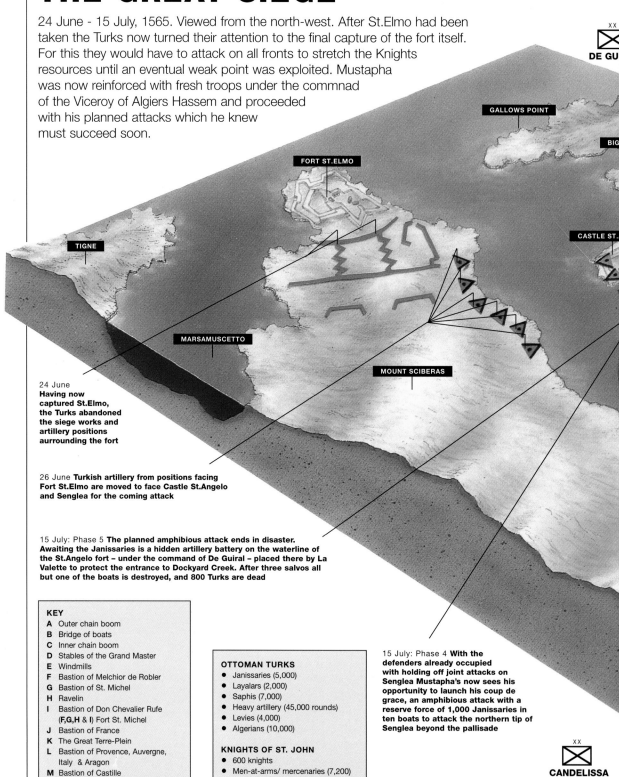

XX
DE GUI

GALLOWS POINT

BIGH

FORT ST.ELMO

CASTLE ST.A

TIGNE

MARSAMUSCETTO

MOUNT SCIBERAS

24 June
Having now captured St.Elmo, the Turks abandoned the siege works and artillery positions aurrounding the fort

26 June Turkish artillery from positions facing Fort St.Elmo are moved to face Castle St.Angelo and Senglea for the coming attack

15 July: Phase 5 The planned amphibious attack ends in disaster. Awaiting the Janissaries is a hidden artillery battery on the waterline of the St.Angelo fort – under the command of De Guiral – placed there by La Valette to protect the entrance to Dockyard Creek. After three salvos all but one of the boats is destroyed, and 800 Turks are dead

15 July: Phase 4 With the defenders already occupied with holding off joint attacks on Senglea Mustapha's now sees his opportunity to launch his coup de grace, an amphibious attack with a reserve force of 1,000 Janissaries in ten boats to attack the northern tip of Senglea beyond the pallisade

XX
CANDELISSA

KEY
A Outer chain boom
B Bridge of boats
C Inner chain boom
D Stables of the Grand Master
E Windmills
F Bastion of Melchior de Robler
G Bastion of St. Michel
H Ravelin
I Bastion of Don Chevalier Rufe
   (**F,G,H** & **I**) Fort St. Michel
J Bastion of France
K The Great Terre-Plein
L Bastion of Provence, Auvergne,
   Italy & Aragon
M Bastion of Castille
N Bastions of Germany & England
O The 'Mole' or harbour front

OTTOMAN TURKS
- Janissaries (5,000)
- Layalars (2,000)
- Saphis (7,000)
- Heavy artillery (45,000 rounds)
- Levies (4,000)
- Algerians (10,000)

KNIGHTS OF ST. JOHN
- 600 knights
- Men-at-arms/ mercenaries (7,200)
- Reinforcements (50 knights and 600
  Spanish infantry)

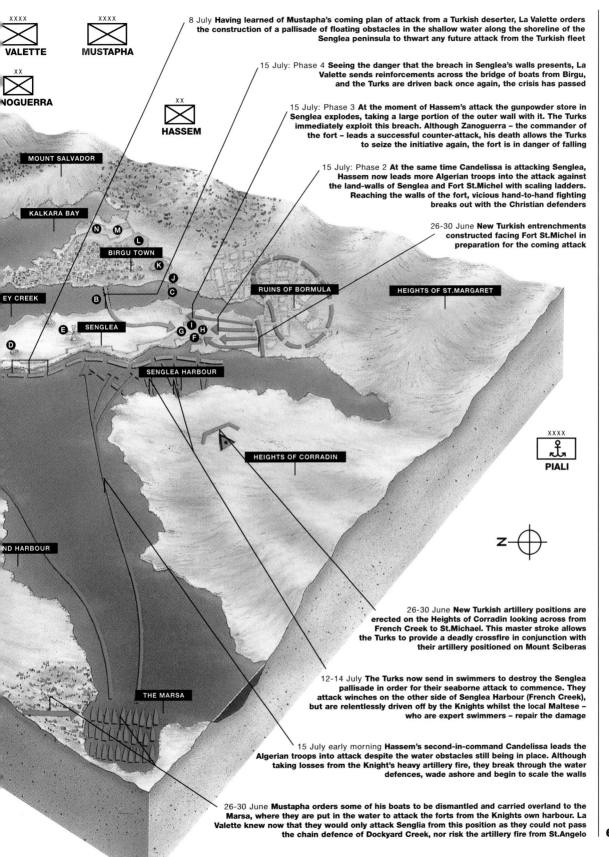

XXXX
VALETTE

XXXX
MUSTAPHA

XX
NOGUERRA

XX
HASSEM

8 July **Having learned of Mustapha's coming plan of attack from a Turkish deserter, La Valette orders the construction of a pallisade of floating obstacles in the shallow water along the shoreline of the Senglea peninsula to thwart any future attack from the Turkish fleet**

15 July: Phase 4 **Seeing the danger that the breach in Senglea's walls presents, La Valette sends reinforcements across the bridge of boats from Birgu, and the Turks are driven back once again, the crisis has passed**

15 July: Phase 3 **At the moment of Hassem's attack the gunpowder store in Senglea explodes, taking a large portion of the outer wall with it. The Turks immediately exploit this breach. Although Zanoguerra – the commander of the fort – leads a successful counter-attack, his death allows the Turks to seize the initiative again, the fort is in danger of falling**

15 July: Phase 2 **At the same time Candelissa is attacking Senglea, Hassem now leads more Algerian troops into the attack against the land-walls of Senglea and Fort St.Michel with scaling ladders. Reaching the walls of the fort, vicious hand-to-hand fighting breaks out with the Christian defenders**

26-30 June **New Turkish entrenchments constructed facing Fort St.Michel in preparation for the coming attack**

MOUNT SALVADOR

KALKARA BAY

N M
L
BIRGU TOWN
K
J
C
B

EY CREEK

E SENGLEA

D

RUINS OF BORMULA

HEIGHTS OF ST.MARGARET

G I H
F

SENGLEA HARBOUR

HEIGHTS OF CORRADIN

XXXX
⚓
PIALI

ND HARBOUR

N ⊕

THE MARSA

26-30 June **New Turkish artillery positions are erected on the Heights of Corradin looking across from French Creek to St.Michael. This master stroke allows the Turks to provide a deadly crossfire in conjunction with their artillery positioned on Mount Sciberas**

12-14 July **The Turks now send in swimmers to destroy the Senglea pallisade in order for their seaborne attack to commence. They attack winches on the other side of Senglea Harbour (French Creek), but are relentlessly driven off by the Knights whilst the local Maltese – who are expert swimmers – repair the damage**

15 July early morning **Hassem's second-in-command Candelissa leads the Algerian troops into attack despite the water obstacles still being in place. Although taking losses from the Knight's heavy artillery fire, they break through the water defences, wade ashore and begin to scale the walls**

26-30 June **Mustapha orders some of his boats to be dismantled and carried overland to the Marsa, where they are put in the water to attack the forts from the Knights own harbour. La Valette knew now that they would only attack Senglia from this position as they could not pass the chain defence of Dockyard Creek, nor risk the artillery fire from St.Angelo**

mine and bring the siege tower forward to take what remained of the parapet. If he made one mistake, it was that in keeping up his bombardment against this one post he tipped his hand as to where the main attack would fall.

It is strange that, even with the Knights in so desperate a situation, Turkish slaves still deserted and joined them. One such did so on 17 August and told La Valette of Mustapha's vow to lead him in chains before Suliman. The Grand Master again addressed the council: "I shall surely prevent him. And even if this siege, contrary to my expectation, should end in a victory for the enemy, I declare to you all that I have resolved that no-one in Constantinople shall ever see a Grand Master of our Holy Order there in chains. If, indeed, the very worst should happen and all be lost, then I intend to put on the uniform of a common soldier and throw myself, sword in hand, into the thick of the enemy and perish there with my children and my brothers."

LA VALETTE STEMS THE TIDE

One thing La Valette had been unable to determine was precisely where the mine had been dug. He would be cautious in the next attack, and he did not have long to wait. The next morning, 18 August, opened with a heavy cannonade on Senglia, and sure enough, as soon as it slackened, the Turks attacked. Mustapha had organised the attack as before – he was commanding at Senglia and Piali at Birgu. While his Iayalars and Janissaries made a fierce assault on St. Michel, Piali sat and waited with his troops.

La Valette was too wily to be caught. Although the garrison at Senglia was hard pressed, he did not send over reinforcements. Finally, in frustration, Mustapha ordered the mine exploded and a vast portion of the defences heaved, crumbled and fell. As the dazed defenders peered into the dust, they saw the onrushing troops of Piali. Their impetus was not to be resisted and the defenders fell back as panic began to spread. The church bell began to ring, signalling that Turks were within the defences, and a chaplain rushed to the Grand Master, shouting: "All is lost! We must retreat to St. Angelo."

La Valette was in his forward command post in Birgu's town square. He was not fully armed, having not yet donned his cuirass or helmet, but his reply to the chaplain was swift and decisive. Picking up a light morrion and grabbing a pike from one of his guards, he ordered his staff to follow him and rushed for the breach. This move stemmed the near rout. Suddenly the Grand Master and senior Knights were joined by other Knights, then soldiers and townspeople. Still at the head of the force, La Valette rushed towards the very breach itself which, although the Turks were retreating, was still occupied by enemy troops. As he approached, a grenade blew up next to him and splinters from it wounded him in the leg. He was urged to withdraw to safety, but the position was not yet secure and he knew that such a move could reverse the situation. As he looked at the now empty breach which still had some enemy flags on it, he replied: "I will not withdraw so long as those banners still wave in the wind. I am seventy one. How is it possible for a man of my age to die more gloriously than in the midst of my friends and

An unarmoured musketeer. His uniform would consist mainly of a coloured overjacket, possibly carrying a coat of arms, and a hat or hat band of distinctive form. The small flasks attached to the shoulder-belt contained the powder for one charge of the musket each. There were usually 12 to a belt, so they acquired the nickname 'apostles'. (*The Army Pageant*, 1900)

brothers, in the service of God?" When the position was reoccupied he had his wounds dressed and then returned to the breach where the captured Turkish flags were presented to him. He ordered them to be hung up in the conventual Church of the Order.

La Valette was right in his supposition that the Turks would renew the attack. As soon as dusk took the sting out of the day's heat the cannonade reopened from all sides, and the attack on the breach was renewed.

Although the sword was the usual weapon of the cavalry soldier and officer, firearms were also used, and not just as a weapon of last resort. In this print the pistol is being cocked in preparation for firing. (Private collection)

With both sides using incendiary devices, there was no trouble seeing the enemy or, indeed, in seeing the Grand Master who had remained in the breach to direct operations. Dawn brought a withdrawal, and for the first time in 24 hours the situation could be assessed. Powder had run low and fresh supplies had to be rushed to the breach. Every bed in the hospital was now full, and the lull was only momentary, as it was obvious that troops were being organised for a renewed attack. The term 'walking wounded' was not used during the siege. It was considered a contradiction in terms: if one could walk one was not wounded! Fighting on 19 August was as vicious as at any time during the siege. Relentless attackers swarmed to the walls and dribbled back, only to swarm again, and that day La Valette suffered a personal loss. Henri de la Valette the Grand Master's nephew and also a Knight of the Order was one of the officers at the Post of Castille. Along with many of the defenders, he was very worried by the siege tower which, although it had yet to be used, posed a severe threat to the walls. During a lull in the attacks, he led out a sally to try to destroy it. Unfortunately, he was wearing particularly fine gilded armour, which made him an instant target for the Turks. He was killed and then a fight ensued for the body, as the Turks wanted the armour as a trophy. Eventually his body was dragged back inside the walls. When told the news, La Valette made the only statement that could be considered in any way despondent during the whole siege: "If the relief from Sicily does not come and we cannot save Malta, we must all die. To the very last man we must bury ourselves beneath these ruins." However, he did not let the death go unavenged, but began directing operations against the tower to bring it down.

The tower was impervious to incendiaries since, though it was made of wood, it was covered with thick sheets of leather which were kept con-

The Turks' decision to build an old-fashioned movable siege tower in an attempt to overcome the defences of Birgu has often been seen as a sign of their desperation. In fact such apparently medieval siege devices still served the Turkish armies well against other foes in Russia and the Middle East. Against modern fortifications such as those at Malta, however, it proved a total failure. The defenders had prepared a secret new artillery position immediately facing the tower's main supports. This was suddenly opened and fired chain shot at the base of the tower, bringing the entire structure crashing down.

stantly wet. Also it was now so close that arquebusiers on the top could, and did, pick off defenders behind the walls, and Janissaries inside the tower could quickly rush out to defend it from attack.

In consulting with his master carpenter, La Valette found that the tower's weak spot was its base. With what in a later age would be called lateral thinking, the Grand Master ordered workmen to begin making a hole in the base of the wall at the very point that the tower was heading for. He ordered that the outer stone not be knocked through until all was prepared. He then had a large cannon brought to the base of the wall and loaded with chain shot. When all was prepared he ordered the wall breached and the cannon run out. In a very short time the tower began to sway and show signs of collapse. Turks began to abandon it, but not all were clear when the last shot smashed its supports and the whole thing came crashing down around them. Immediately the hole in the wall was repaired preventing Turkish reprisals.

At almost the same time that this was happening, Mustapha was attacking Senglia again with another device. From its description it seems to have been a kind of sealed petard which was to be used to further reduce a section of the defensive wall that, although not fully breached, was so ruined as to form slopes on either side. It was carried forward and up the wall during an attack then rolled down the inner wall where it came to rest at the defenders' feet. In a moment that might have been scripted by Hollywood, the defenders saw that the fuse had been cut too long and so rolled it back up the ramp and over the wall where it bounced into the ditch behind which the Turks were waiting to attack after it exploded. Explode it did, but right in the faces of the attackers. The bomb certainly had an anti-personnel quality, as shrapnel tore into the Turks and killed many. The defenders immediately attacked, and the Turks fled. From their darkest hours the Knights had emerged undefeated with victory almost a possibilty.

Here the pistol is levelled at the target and fired. Note that the hand is twisted so that the lock plate faces upwards. This (hopefully) ensured that the powder was resting over the touch hole when ignited and so detonated the charge in the barrel. (Private collection)

TURKISH TROUBLES

For the first time serious doubts were beginning to form in Turkish minds. If their victory really was the will of Allah, why were all their efforts failing? The troops were more and more unwilling to attack, surrounded as they were by dead, with the stench of rotting bodies wafting into their tents at night. They were already suffering from dysentery, and they feared the onset of plague. Worse, their supplies were becoming depleted because their ships were being captured by Christian vessels and because some captains just did not want to return. Mustapha had another problem: if he did not leave within the next four weeks, he would have to winter on the island, and after mid-September the winds would not be favourable to make the 1,000-mile journey back to Constantinople. One thing he did know was that however bad his supplies were, the Christians' supplies were worse, and if he stayed on the island, he would certainly take it.

Piali forbade the project. There were no repair facilities on the island and the harbours, which were fine in summer, would be unsuitable in winter. He would not permit the Sultan's fleet to remain so exposed. With Dragut gone, the hostility between the co-commanders flared: Mustapha saw that Piali's pettifogging concern for his ships and incompetence in keeping the island had cost him men and time; now it looked as if it might cost him the campaign.

The situation in the Christian camp was even more desperate, and there was still no sign of relief.

REASSESSMENT

Whatever troubles the Turks were having it was not immediately evident to the defenders. The attack was renewed with equal vigour on 20 August – 8,000 Turks under the Sanjak Cheder attacking St. Michel. Cheder had vowed to take the fort or die in the attempt, and his personal bodyguard had vowed to join him. The Sanjak at least kept his vow. Marked out by his fine robes, he became an immediate target for the defenders' muskets and he fell at the head of his troops. Now it was the Muslims who were fighting to prevent the body of an officer falling into the hands of the enemy. Into this fight lunged Chevalier Juan de la Cerda, the Knight who had made the early pessimistic report on the state of St. Elmo and had ever since lived under the cloud of being thought a coward. This day the cloud was blown away for ever as he plunged almost alone into the thick of the Janissaries surrounding the Sanjak's body and was eventually cut down.

Meanwhile, at Birgu a second tower had been prepared and was being used against what remained of the bastion of Castile. This time the base of the tower had been reinforced with earth and stone to prevent it

LEFT **Another view of a siege tower in action. The leather hides with which it is covered would be soaked in water to help prevent the tower being burnt and the tower itself had to be pushed forward on a roadway made of logs if the ground was not smooth enough or was in any way boggy. In the illustration fascines have been thrown into a water-filled moat and the roadway laid on top of that. In Malta that was one problem the Turks did not have to contend with. (Historical Military Productions, New Orleans)**

THE GREAT SIEGE

16 July - 7 August. Viewed from the north-west. Surrounding the garrison on all sides with their artillery train, the Turks being to systematically pound it in preparation for the coming final assaults. However, the planned Turkish attacks falter amid the carnage of St. Michel and Birgu and there near success is thwarted by a surprise attack from the Mdina garrison who destroy the Turkish camp just at their moment of triumph

GALLOWS POINT

BIGH

FORT ST.ELMO

15 July-7 August **Turkish artillery position on Gallows Point is redirected and strengthened, a constant cannonade is now directed towards the Christians night and day**

CASTLE S

TIGNE

MARSAMUSCETTO

MOUNT SCIBERAS

19 July **Once the debris has been partially cleared, the Turks also position artillery in St.Elmo itself. They now enforce a deadly cross-fire from all points surrounding the garrison**

16 July **The siege works and artillery placements facing Fort St.Elmo are now completely abandoned**

17 July **Camouflaged artillery positions situated on the edge of Mount Sceberas to pound the defences whilst the Turkish sappers do work around St.Angelo and St.Michael**

2 August **The fiercest bombardment of the whole siege takes place, so loud that it is heard over 100 miles away. Every point of the defences comes under fire, St.Angelo itself is in a deadly cross-fire from Mount Salvador, Gallows Point, Mount Sciberas and the captured St.Elmo. This is followed by a major all-out Turkish assault which lasts for six hours until they are driven off. Mustapha responds by ordering a 5-day bombardment of the garrison in preparation for the next attack**

KEY
A Outer chain boom
B Bridge of boats
C Inner chain boom
D Stables of the Grand Master
E Windmills
F Bastion of Melchior de Robler
G Bastion of St. Michel
H Ravelin
I Bastion of Don Chevalier Rufe
   (**F,G,H & I**) Fort St. Michel
J Bastion of France
K The Great Terre-Plein
L Bastion of Provence, Auvergne,
   Italy & Aragon
M Bastion of Castille
N Bastions of Germany & England
O The 'Mole' or harbour front

OTTOMAN TURKS
● Janissaries (4,000)
● Layalars (1,800)
● Saphis (6,500)
● Heavy artillery (30,000 rounds)
● Levies (3,500)
● Algerians (7,500)

KNIGHTS OF ST. JOHN
● 500 knights
● Men-at-arms/ mercenaries (6,000)

CANDELISSA

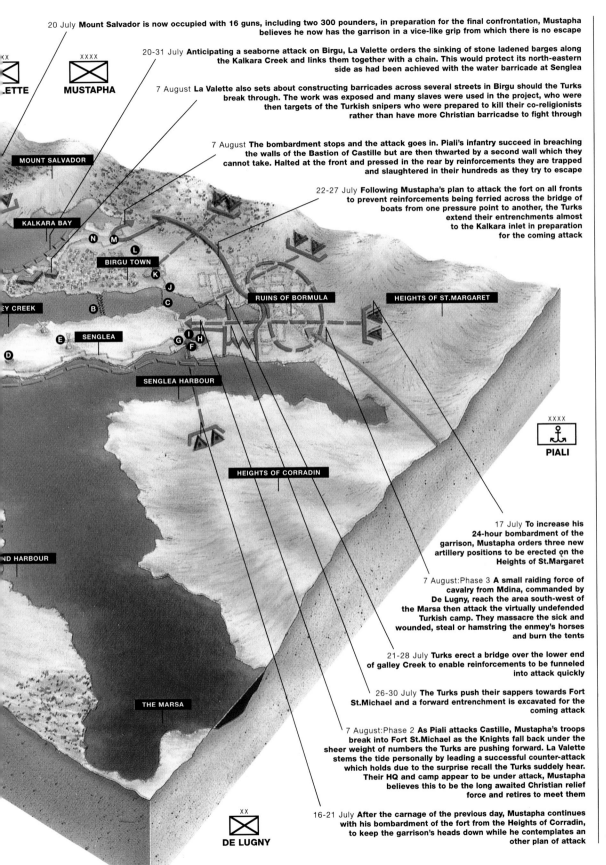

20 July Mount Salvador is now occupied with 16 guns, including two 300 pounders, in preparation for the final confrontation, Mustapha believes he now has the garrison in a vice-like grip from which there is no escape

20-31 July Anticipating a seaborne attack on Birgu, La Valette orders the sinking of stone ladened barges along the Kalkara Creek and links them together with a chain. This would protect its north-eastern side as had been achieved with the water barricade at Senglea

7 August La Valette also sets about constructing barricades across several streets in Birgu should the Turks break through. The work was exposed and many slaves were used in the project, who were then targets of the Turkish snipers who were prepared to kill their co-religionists rather than have more Christian barricadse to fight through

7 August The bombardment stops and the attack goes in. Piali's infantry succeed in breaching the walls of the Bastion of Castille but are then thwarted by a second wall which they cannot take. Halted at the front and pressed in the rear by reinforcements they are trapped and slaughtered in their hundreds as they try to escape

22-27 July Following Mustapha's plan to attack the fort on all fronts to prevent reinforcements being ferried across the bridge of boats from one pressure point to another, the Turks extend their entrenchments almost to the Kalkara inlet in preparation for the coming attack

MOUNT SALVADOR

KALKARA BAY

N M

L

BIRGU TOWN

K

J

EY CREEK

B

C

RUINS OF BORMULA

HEIGHTS OF ST.MARGARET

E

SENGLEA

D

G I H

F

SENGLEA HARBOUR

XXXX

PIALI

HEIGHTS OF CORRADIN

ND HARBOUR

17 July To increase his 24-hour bombardment of the garrison, Mustapha orders three new artillery positions to be erected on the Heights of St.Margaret

7 August:Phase 3 A small raiding force of cavalry from Mdina, commanded by De Lugny, reach the area south-west of the Marsa then attack the virtually undefended Turkish camp. They massacre the sick and wounded, steal or hamstring the enmey's horses and burn the tents

21-28 July Turks erect a bridge over the lower end of galley Creek to enable reinforcements to be funneled into attack quickly

26-30 July The Turks push their sappers towards Fort St.Michael and a forward entrenchment is excavated for the coming attack

7 August:Phase 2 As Piali attacks Castille, Mustapha's troops break into Fort St.Michael as the Knights fall back under the sheer weight of numbers the Turks are pushing forward. La Valette stems the tide personally by leading a successful counter-attack which holds due to the surprise recall the Turks suddenly hear. Their HQ and camp appear to be under attack, Mustapha believes this to be the long awaited Christian relief force and retires to meet them

THE MARSA

16-21 July After the carnage of the previous day, Mustapha continues with his bombardment of the fort from the Heights of Corradin, to keep the garrison's heads down while he contemplates an other plan of attack

XX

DE LUGNY

XXXX

MUSTAPHA

ETTE

75

sharing the fate of its sister structure. As it came on, its snipers began to pin down the defenders and it soon became obvious that in this position they would be unable to properly defend the breach from a renewed attack. La Valette set the engineers to digging at the base of the wall again. This time when the stones were knocked out, two Knights led out a party of men-at-arms and soldiers, who clambered up the tower's stone base and up to the top, killing those that did not run away. Immediately a party of picked gunners with two cannon appeared from the wall, and the Turkish tower was turned into an outwork of the defences, with the Knights and men-at-arms protecting the gunners from Turkish raids. Perhaps it was the sinking morale of the enemy that allowed this operation to succeed; certainly Christian morale was high, and they still had spies in the enemy camp. Later in the day an arrow was shot into Birgu. Its message was short and to the point: "Thursday".

STAND OR RETREAT

On the evening of 23 August the Grand Council of the Order of St. John of Jerusalem, of Rhodes and of Malta met. Also in attendance were all the Knights Grand Cross. Each Knight gave his assessment of the situation and opinion. The consensus was that the defences of Birgu could no longer be held, that the walls were so riddled with mines and countermines that they could collapse at any moment. Indeed, in order to prevent a similar disaster to the explosion of the great mine at the Post of Castille, the defenders had been countermining vigorously. Occasionally they broke through into the Turkish mines and fierce hand-to-hand battles with picks and shovels took place. Now was the time to retreat, take the archives and relics of the Order from the conventual church and make a last stand at St. Angelo.

There was only one dissenting voice to this opinion, but that was the voice of Jean Parisot de la Valette the Grand Master. "I respect your advice, my brethren, but I shall not take it. And these are my reasons. If we abandon Birgu we lose Senglia, for the garrison there can not hold out on its own. The fortress of St. Angelo is too small to hold all the population as well as ourselves and our men. And I have no intention of abandoning the loyal Maltese, their wives and their children to the enemy. St. Angelo's water supply, even supposing that we can get all the people within its walls, will not be adequate. With the Turks masters of Senglia and occupying the ruins of Birgu, it will only be a matter of time before the strong walls of St. Angelo will fall before their concentrated fire. At the moment they are forced to divert their energies and fire power. Such will not be the case if we and all our men are locked within St. Angelo. No, my brothers this and this only is the place where we must stand and fight. Here we must all perish together, or finally, with the help of God, succeed in driving off our enemy."

As for the relics, particularly the hand of John the Baptist, La Valette was of the opinion that their removal would cause despondency in the hearts of the defenders. Of course the records of the Order might as well stay, in that if the battle were lost, there would be no need for them. The decision was accepted. In order to impress his commitment on the native Maltese of Senglia and Birgu, he left only sufficient troops in St. Angelo to man the guns; the rest joined the outer defences. He then blew up the drawbridge that connected St. Angelo to Birgu. There would be no abandonment, no retreat and no surrender.

CRISIS FOR THE TURKS

A Turkish artillery officer sits dejectedly by his guns after a siege that has dismounted at least one of his pieces. (Historical Military Productions, New Orleans)

The invaders had arrived with ample stores and more than enough powder and ammunition for a four-week siege – the projected length of the campaign – but now everything was running low. The wisdom of bringing all the livestock within the walls and even harvesting the green crops before the Turks arrived was evident. The Turks could not sustain themselves on the island and had to order supplies from North Africa. Daylong cannonades were a thing of the past, and heavy bombardments were reserved for the prelude to attacks. Some of the guns were even becoming unserviceable through constant use, and though Mustapha tried to withdraw them from the batteries as unobtrusively as possible, the defenders had noticed both the withdrawal and the slackening of fire. There was still powder and guns on the fleet, but it is a measure of how Turkish confidence had been shaken that these were not used, because it was accepted that if the fleet did withdraw before winter, it might have to fight its way back to Constantinople

Worse was to come. Mustapha had been expecting a large supply ship from North Africa, but he now received news that it had been attacked and captured en route. His chief quartermaster informed him that they had only enough flour for 25 days; in other words, if they were to withdraw at that very moment, they would still have to go on short rations in order to reach home. What could be a more demoralising prospect for an army in which the officers' rank titles were based on culinary designations and a regiment's most prized possession was its cooking pot?

More ships were immediately sent for supplies, and Mustapha considered his options. He ordered the mining of the walls of Birgu to continue at an accelerated pace and then he decided to carry out what he had intended to do when he first arrived – capture Mdina. If this seems a desperate act, it is difficult to fault his logic. If he were to winter in Malta, he would have to take it anyway. In spite of his vast troop losses, he still had thousands more men than the Christians, but with demoralisation spreading through the Turkish host, it would be better to attack sooner rather than later. There were also other advantages for him. He would be able to use the cannon of Mdina to replace the guns that were now unserviceable, and if in the end he were forced to withdraw, at least he could claim to have captured the capital of the island.

ARRIVAL OF THE RELIEF FORCE AND THE DEPARTURE OF THE TURKS

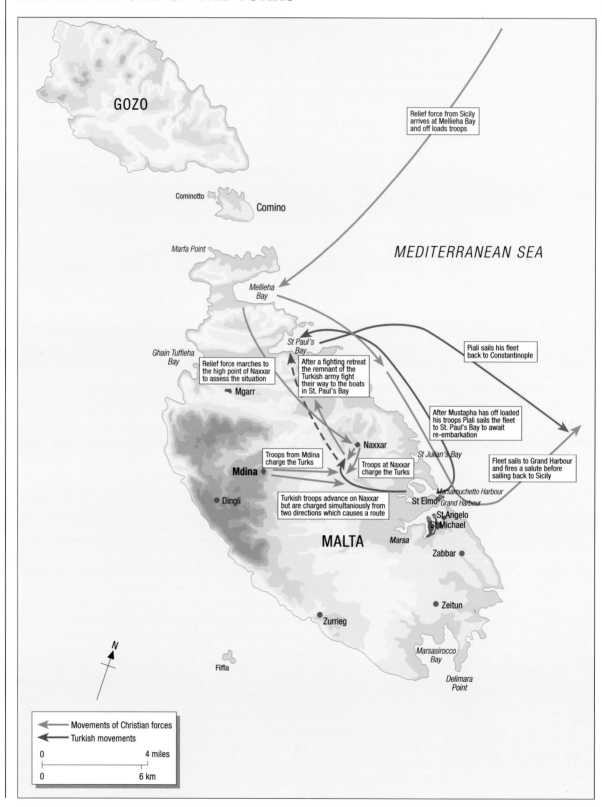

GOZO

Cominotto

Comino

Marfa Point

MEDITERRANEAN SEA

Mellieha Bay

Relief force from Sicily arrives at Mellieha Bay and off loads troops

Ghain Tuffieha Bay

St Paul's Bay

Relief force marches to the high point of Naxxar to assess the situation

After a fighting retreat the remnant of the Turkish army fight their way to the boats in St. Paul's Bay

Piali sails his fleet back to Constantinople

Mgarr

After Mustapha has off loaded his troops Piali sails the fleet to St. Paul's Bay to await re-embarkation

Naxxar

St Julian's Bay

Troops from Mdina charge the Turks

Troops at Naxxar charge the Turks

Fleet sails to Grand Harbour and fires a salute before sailing back to Sicily

Mdina

Marsamuchetto Harbour

St Elmo Grand Harbour

Dingli

Turkish troops advance on Naxxar but are charged simultaniously from two directions which causes a route

St Angelo
St Michael

MALTA Marsa

Zabbar

Marsasirocco Bay

N

Zeitun

Zurrieg

Filfla

Delimara Point

Movements of Christian forces
Turkish movements

0 _____ 4 miles

0 _____ 6 km

Citta Notabile, as Mdina was originally called, had been the capital since the Romans ruled Malta. It was here that the governor Publius had given shelter to St. Paul, and on the site of his house stood a cathedral that was the centre of faith on the island. Despite all this, it was still somewhat small to be called a city. However, Birgu was only a small town and Senglia barely a village. Ironically Mdina's defences were Arabic, built during the Muslim occupation which had lasted for 200 years before the island had been captured by Count Roger of Normandy, 500 years earlier.

Spies in the Turkish camp and troop movements in his direction alerted the Chevalier don Mesquita, Mdina's governor, to the danger. Don Mesquita was a clever man. He had proved this many times during the siege, sending out the Order's cavalry to raid and harass the Turks. Up to now his most clever strategy had been to raid the Turkish camp and, by convincing them the relief force had arrived, snatching victory at St. Michel from Mustapha's grasp. He knew that if the Turks made a determined assault, he would not be able to hold them. Apart from the cavalry, which were few enough, he had a very small garrison, very little powder and shot, and a town whose walls looked impressive but were old and all but crumbling. What he did have in abundance were civilians, since the native population had retreated there when the Turks had arrived; it was full of Maltese.

There were some elements in his favour: the city was built on a promontory which made it look impressive and meant it was only approachable on one side; he had lots of uniforms; and he was desperate. Don Mesquita issued arms and uniforms to all the peasants and had them stand on the battlements. He brought all his arquebusiers and cannon to the wall he expected the Turks to assault, and then he waited.

The story had gone out among the Turks that Mdina was almost undefended, weak and would give them no trouble. After all, if there had been fresh troops there, why had they not relieved their brethren? As the Turkish troops made their way up the long shallow slope, they saw their objective silhouetted against the skyline. Scouts sent out beforehand returned to tell their officers that even the walls that could not be assaulted were bristling with soldiers and cannon. With difficulty the officers urged their men on, and then halted out of range of the guns to plan the assault. Amazingly, Mdina opened fire on them. Cannon roared and muskets crackled. They were not even in range. A few cannon balls rolled to a halt before reaching the formation. They could not have done more damage if they had killed half the men there: the rumour immediately spread that this was another St. Elmo, that here were fresh troops behind thick walls with so much powder they could afford to waste it. Messengers were sent back to Mustapha that here was no ripe plum but another month-long siege at best, and the orders came back to withdraw. News of the withdrawal soon reached the defenders of Senglia and Birgu. They were now beginning to believe that, even without help they might actually be able to win!

RELIEF AT LAST

The intensity of the siege and his lack of trust in the Viceroy's promises had served to cut the Grand Master off from news of events in Sicily from late August, but things had taken a turn for the better.

There were now 200 Knights of the Order with their own men-at-arms and soldiers in Messina. They had had enough of Don Garcea's procrastination and had progressed from pleas to be transported to Malta, through demands that were fast becoming threats. During one interview, with Chevalier Louis de Lastic, Grand Prior of Auvergne, Don Garcea was affronted that he was not being give his title of 'Excellency'. Lastic replied: "Sire, provided that we arrive in Malta in time to save the religion, I will give you what titles you please, 'Excellency', 'Your Highness', or even, if you wish, 'Your Majesty'!" Don Garcea's reply was that it was not enough to send a relief force: that relief must be successful, and 8,000 men was a pitifully small band to send against 40,000 Turks. However, on 22 August he had held a review of the troops so far assembled and finally on 25 August 28 galleys put to sea carrying something over 9,000 men bound for Malta. Unfortunately, they were hit by a summer gale and forced to turn back. The fleet regrouped at the island of Favingana, off the Sicilian port of Marsala, where it undertook temporary repairs before returning to Linosa to complete repair and re-embark.

Don Garcea found La Valette's last message waiting for him. The south of the island and both main harbours were occupied, it said, so he suggested that the Viceroy land his troops at Mgarr or Mellieha. Both of these bays had sandy beaches ideal for troop landings, and both were reasonably sheltered.

On 4 September the fleet set out again, Chevalier Don Cordona commanding the van, with Don Garcea in command of the main body. Bad weather struck again, but through the heavy conditions and thickening mist Don Cordona pressed on to Gozo; predictably Don Garcea returned to Sicily. With the fleet thus separated, it would have been an ideal time for Piali to attack and destroy the ships of the advance guard. Surprisingly he did not.

A variety of Ottoman Janissary troops depicted in the *Súleymanname*. Although the majority wear the white cap associated with Cemaat units, the two at the bottom left of the picture have the distinctive red cap of the Silâhtar guard corps, which normally fought as cavalry. All would have featured heavily during the weeks of battle. (Ms. Haz. 1597-8, f.113a, Topkapi Lib., Istanbul)

From 24 August there was a week-long lull in the fighting. A steady cannonade was continued as before, and then on 1 September there was a mass assault on Senglia and Birgu once more. This was not an assault like the previous one – the heart had gone out of the attackers, as if they had accepted that their victory was not 'the will of Allah'. Mustapha and Piali were like desperate gamblers, throwing good money after bad and trying to win a game with the cards against them. They knew only too well that Suliman the Magnificent did not have a forgiving nature.

The demands of the Knights on Don Garcea were beginning to verge on the aggressive. This latest move almost seemed calculated to make the relief of Malta fail. Finally, he gave in, the fleet was reunited and on 6 September they dropped anchor in Mellieha Bay. The next morning the landing began, and news of it spread quickly over the island. Reports vary, but there were probably about 10,000 in all, hardly enough to make any difference if the Turks had been in good heart, for they still outnumbered the Christians more than two to one, but the Turks were already beaten.

La Valette decided to play another card. He contrived to have one of the Muslim slaves working in his countermines overhear some officers talking of the 16,000 troops that were even now landing under the command of the Viceroy of Sicily. It was then contrived that the slave escape and reach the Turkish lines safely. As La Valette had hoped, the story was repeated to Mustapha, who was told that the Knights were jubilant. With glum resignation he ordered the evacuation of the island.

Even now Piali did not move his fleet. The anchorage of Mellieha was good but exposed, and if he had attacked he could have done great

In complete contrast to the print showing an attack on the Bastion of Castile, the print showing the arrival of the Christian relief force on 7 September 1565 is more of a stylised map. The galleys and transport stream in at the left of the picture, while tightly packed units of infantrymen march across bare hills to a fort flying the flag of the Knights. (Via Dr. David Chandler)

damage to the galleys of Don Garcea. As it was, they unloaded and left without molestation. In an uncharacteristic show of gallantry, Don Garcea sailed past the mouths of Grand Harbour and Marasirocco still crammed with Piali's squadrons. He fired a triple gun salute to the flag of the Order and each successive Christian ship with him did the same, before peeling off and heading back to Sicily to transport back the 4,000 new troops that were waiting. It is indicative of the Turks' morale that Piali made no move against them, even though with the forces at his disposal not a single Christian ship should have been allowed to reach the island, let alone leave it.

THE FINAL BLUNDER

La Valette's thoughts had turned from resignation of a fight to the death to the possibility of recouping some of his losses. All during the night he had hoped to hear from the relief force so that he could plan a joint venture to prevent the Turks removing all of their cannon and shot, so that he could add them to his own depleted arsenal. All he heard were the obvious sounds of an army in retreat, of cannon being hauled from their positions and prepared for embarkation. The camp was being struck, and the detached squadrons were massing to join the fleet when it left the anchorage of Marsamuschetto. The evacuation was not delayed. Anything that could not easily be dismantled was left where it stood, including the siege towers and even a few of the heaviest guns.

The relief force marched straight for Mdina, and after making contact with the garrison, moved to the west to the village of Naxxar, which occupies the top of a steep rise. The marshal of the force, Ascanio de la Corna, was an experienced soldier, famed not only in his native Italy but by his reputation in many other countries too. He was not about to risk any of his men until he knew precisely where the enemy were and what they were about. He waited until dawn.

At first light, scouts were sent out of Senglia and Birgu. An unbelievable sight met the eyes of the defenders who looked out over the walls on 8 September: empty trenches and gun emplacements, not a single enemy flag to be seen, no cannonade, no wailing Turkish music; just the wreck and devastation of a battlefield strewn with the debris of retreat. After four months the Turks had gone.

Some of the Knights rode up to St. Elmo, which although only a crumbling ruin, was clean and fresh, since the putrefying corpses that abounded at Senglia and Birgu had long since been swept away from there. What can have been the feelings of the Knights who entered that place on that day? The first Christians there since the glorious defence that had saved the island but cost the lives of all of the Order that were there. Whatever they thought, they knew what to do. One of them withdrew a large folded red cloth from his saddle-bag, attached it to the halyard and ran it up the flagpole. As it snapped open in the wind, it displayed on its field the white eight-pointed cross of the Order. As they left Malta, the Turks would see that St. Elmo was once more a fortress of the Order. Everything they had gained in four months of hard fighting had been lost in less than 24 hours. To emphasise the point, light cannon were brought up to the fort so that St. Elmo would have the honour of

THE TURKISH RETREAT
Evacuating an army by sea was just as difficult and dangerous in the 16th century as in any other period of history. Harried by the defending army and by the relief force from Sicily, the Turks struggled to maintain cohesion. Meanwhile their courageous commander Mustapha Pasha remained with the rearguard to protect the evacuation. In fact it was here, during their final retreat, that the discipline of the Ottoman Empire's mixed force of Turks, Arabs, North Africans, Balkan Muslims and others, showed what a remarkable army it really was – despite its crushing defeat on the island of Malta.

firing the last shots at the enemies of the 'Holy Religion'.

At the same hour that the alarm bell normally sounded in Birgu, the bells of the conventual church of St. Lawrence rang out, calling the defenders to mass on the feast of the Nativity of the Virgin. It is said that there are no atheists in a foxhole; the faith of the Knights and islanders must have been confirmed beyond measure as they gave thanks to God for their miraculous deliverance, while around them defensive walls still collapsed as the honeycomb of mines gave way here and there.

As his army was embarking, Mustapha received startling news from the scouts he had sent out to report on the relief force: only 28 ships had arrived and perhaps 8,000 men had landed. He immediately ordered his troops to disembark and engage the enemy. Piali protested and a furious row broke out between the two, which ended in the uneasy compromise that some troops would be landed but the fleet would leave and wait at St. Paul's bay to pick them up. That way Mustapha might claim one last victory but Piali would be in no position to remain, so that his longed-for departure was assured.

When La Valette heard of what was happening, he immediately sent warning to de la Corna at Naxxar. Mustapha had landed about 9,000 men, and if he was able to defeat the relief force, that might put fresh heart into the Turks. If he then decided to spend the winter on the island, Malta could still be lost.

De la Corna held his men on the high ground in the classic fashion. He did not want to give the Turks any chance to beat him on the plain. He would make their advance as difficult as possible. De la Corna was explaining the strategy to his officers as the Turks marched up the road toward him, but the Knights of the Order were in no mood to listen. "There is the enemy! And there in the distance are the smoking ruins where our brethren died!" Turning their horses to face the enemy, they charged at full tilt. Troops began to follow, and realising that it would be impossible to stop them, De la Corna gave the order to charge. Observing all this were the cavalry and militia from Mdina who had formed up in front of the city, to the west of Naxxar. Seeing what was happening, they too charged without orders. If anyone commanded on that day, it was God, for no-one (other than de la Corna, accepting the inevitable) gave any orders, yet the attack was flawless. As the relief force hit the Turks head-on, the Mdina garrison swept across the plain and took the flank.

Even before the attacks reached their target the Turks began to break. Allah had made his decision known: they had been about to go home and now they were brought back for a fight they knew they must lose. It was Mustapha's worst decision of the campaign. All his other plans had at least had the chance of success, but this was doomed from the start. All he could do now was fight his way to St. Paul's bay.

The panic among the Turks became a near rout. The Spahis and all the cavalry made a run for St. Paul's bay, and the only group that held the situation together were the Janissaries around Mustapha. Certainly Mustapha was no coward – he had proved that many times in the siege – but ironically he proved it best on this day. From being in the van of the army he began to organise a rear-guard. Two horses were killed from under him, and once he was only saved from capture by a Janissary counter-attack. One group of Turks bravely defended a small watchtower on a small rise from where they could help protect their army's flank, but eventually they were dislodged and the advance continued. As the Turks neared St. Paul's Bay, they had outrun the Christian infantry and the cavalry was strung out. The exertion was tremendous: four Knights died of heat stroke in their armour, but still they pressed on, leaving the infantry far behind. Mustapha halted his Janissary arquebusiers and ordered them to turn and fire on the Knights to buy his force more time. Several Knights were wounded and unhorsed, including Alvarez de Sande, who had led the attack, and the pursuit faltered.

A further Turkish defence was arranged by Hassem, Dragut's son, who had taken no active part in the command of the siege since he had failed to make good his boast to take Senglia. He placed groups of arquebusiers behind the rocks, bushes and hillocks surrounding the bay. Again the Knights and men-at-arms were checked but only momentarily. When the infantry caught up with them, they pushed forward together and forced their way down to the bay. Fighting continued even into the water, and Christians on shore traded shots with Muslims on board ships. The confusion and carnage in the bay was indescribable. Not surprisingly, Mustapha Pasha was in one of the last boats to leave the shore, but go he did, never to return.

Though dating from the battle of Abukir, during Napoleon's Egyptian campaign, this scene almost mirrors the scene at St. Paul's bay, as the defeated Turks plunge headlong into the sea in a desperate attempt to save themselves.

AFTERMATH

One of the most dramatic illustrations in the magnificent *Süleymanname* manuscript, made in 1558, shows Ottoman forces overrunning a river fortress on the frontier of the Hapsburg Empire in central Europe. This was the kind of siege warfare in which the elite Janissary infantry excelled. (Ms. Haz. 1517, Topkapi Lib., Istanbul)

The robe of a Knight of the Sovereign Military Order of Malta, as worn today. (Author's photograph)

The first priority for Mustapha and Piali now was to save their heads. Suliman did not take defeat well, and this was more than defeat – it was humiliation. They sent the report of what had happened back to Constantinople in the fastest galley, so that his anger would have had time to cool before they arrived. It was a good move. In the end, Suliman philosophically said that he now understood that it was only in his own hand that his 'sword' was invincible. He sent word back to the fleet that they must arrive and land the troops at night, so that the people would not witness the shame in which they returned. He vowed also: "Next year, I myself, the Sultan Suliman, will lead an expedition against that accursed island. I will not spare one single inhabitant!" This was not to be. Having renewed his attacks in Hungary, he died the next year, on 15 September 1566, while directing the siege of Szigetvar at the age of 72. In 1571 Turkish plans for world conquest were finally brought to an end at the battle of Lepanto. In that battle the only Turk to distinguish himself was El Louck Aly, governor of Alexandria, who had been present at Malta. On this last occasion that the oared galley predominated, he even succeeded in out-manoeuvring the famed admiral Andrea Doria, thereby saving his squadron. The rest of the Turkish commanders sank into obscurity. Thus began the decline of the Ottoman Empire.

Also at the great Christian victory of Lapanto was the Chevalier Romegas, perhaps the finest seaman of the Order at any time in their history. But many of his confreres of the siege had already died, spent in the rigours of the defence. It was as if the very island were worn out with the fight. However, the Grand Master would not let it rest: he knew that if the attack were renewed, they must be ready, so throughout Europe the word went out and the money flowed in. Not only were the old defences reconstructed, and in a stronger fashion, but new ones went up – in particular a new city on the heights of Mount Sciberas, on the very site of the Turkish artillery batteries. Never again would an enemy be able to use that position to fire into the forts. The new city was built with thick walls and every modern defence, for a siege that never came. It had a fine cathedral dedicated to St. John and it was named after the Grand Master Jean Parisot de la Valette – Valetta.

Lascaris, the Greek of princely heritage who had deserted the Turks, brought such valuable information and been so useful during the siege, was granted a pension for life by La Valette.

The Grand Master never condemned nor complained about Don Garcea de Toledo, Viceroy of Sicily, though his sluggish performance could easily have lost the siege. Perhaps the memory of the gallant death of Don Garcea's son prevented him. Whatever the reasons for Don Garcea's tardiness, he was removed from his position by the king and died in obscurity.

Pope Pius V offered La Valette the 'Red Hat', but he already

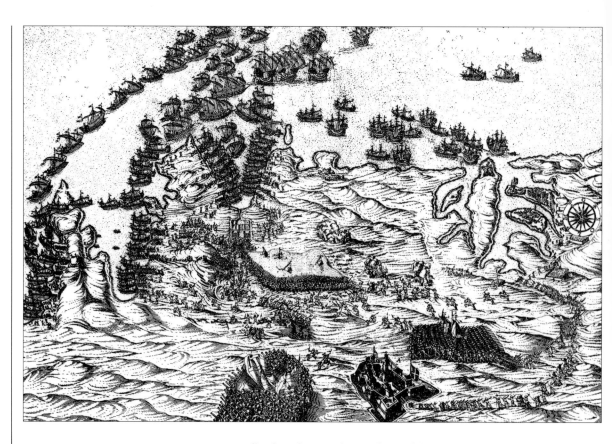

The flight and departure of the Ottoman army from Malta on 13 September 1565, on an Italian print. At the centre a tightly packed formation of Ottoman troops makes its way towards the ships in the bay to the left, harried all the way by Christian infantry and cavalry. Two other Christian formations close in from the right and from the base of the picture. In the background the Ottoman Turkish fleet, mostly consisting of galleys but also including large sailing transports, sets out on its return journey to Istanbul. (Via Dr. David Chandler)

was a cardinal and accepting to be ordained one by His Holiness would only have served to embroil the Order in Vatican politics. During the remaining three years of his life La Valette oversaw the construction of the new defences, ran the council, and received ambassadors to his tiny but most significant state. In July 1568 he spent a day hawking in the summer sun. That evening he suffered a stroke. For the remaining weeks of his life he continued to put his affairs in order, while every day growing a little weaker. Finally on 21 August 1568, he died. Quite literally an age came to an end: the last of the Crusader Knights, whose name could be ranked among any in history, had joined his god. The holy land might be lost for ever, but Europe would never be Muslim. His epitaph was written by Sir Oliver Starkey, his friend and secretary: "Here lies La Valette, worthy of eternal honour. He who was once the scourge of Africa and Asia, and the shield of Europe, whence he expelled the barbarians by his holy arms, the first to be buried in this beloved city, whose founder he was." When the cathedral of St. John was completed La Valette's body was laid in the crypt and in due time so was that of Sir Oliver.

The impact of the result of the siege on Europe is probably best expressed by the English sovereign at the time, the arch Protestant Elizabeth I. During the siege she wrote: "If the Turks should prevail against the Isle of Malta, it is uncertain what further peril might follow to the rest of Christendom." When news of the victory reached England, she ordered the Archbishop of Canterbury to give thanks in a special service three times a week for six weeks. It is ironic that if Sir Oliver Starkey or the other two Englishmen who fought in the siege had visited their homeland, they could well have been put to death for their faith.

MALTA AND THE ORDER TODAY

The Great Siege was of course not the last siege of Malta: in World War Two, while it was part of the British Empire, once again the island defied invasion and the people were collectively awarded the George Cross (the civilian equivalent of the VC), which is still displayed on the national flag.

Although little of the original defences from the time of the siege remain, some of the buildings do, including the conventual church in Birgu and the core of the structure at St. Angelo. There are also the armouries and museums on the island, which have many items dating from the siege, particularly the monstrous cannon balls that were used by the Turks.

The Order continues today in almost every country of the world and in number of members is stronger than ever. However, there was a time when it seemed as if the Order might die out. When Napoleon was on his way to invade Egypt he stopped in Malta and took the island. With virtually no show of resistance, the Knights handed over their fiefdom and left. The Knights of the late 18th century were mainly old, and living on a long-dead reputation, but this new exile put a spark of defiance into them that was to give them the spur to survive. In desperation, a group of the Knights offered the Grand Mastership to Czar Paul of Russia, who was not, of course, even Catholic. The Order today still suffers as a result, since many bogus orders have sprung up claiming descent from the Russian 'Orthodox' branch of the Order. This is, of course, a fiction. The remnants of the Order finally came to reside in Rome, where the headquarters remain today. Many imitation orders have sprung up pretending to be the 'true' Order but of course there is only one Sovereign Military Order of Malta, as it is commonly known today.

Recently the island of Malta and the Order have had talks, and it is certainly not beyond the bounds of possibility that the Order might return to the island – not as overlords but as honoured guests whose work is recognised throughout the world. The Knights of today still fight for the faith, but not with sword, cannon and lance. They do so with medical volunteers, medevac helicopters and hospitals. Because they are still recognised as 'sovereign', they exchange ambassadors with the nations of the world and are thus able to use their influence for good at the highest level and per-

BELOW **The present Prince Grand Master of the Sovereign Military Order of Malta, His Most Eminent Highness, Fra. Andrew Bertie (centre), the first English Grand Master in 700 years. The term 'Fra' is short for Frater, or brother. All members with this title (which include all the senior members of Council) have taken full religious vows of poverty, chastity and obedience.**

Knights of the Order of Malta attending mass during the pilgrimage to Lourdes which the Order undertakes every year.

Prelates, Knights and affiliates of the Order escorting the Blessed Sacrament in solemn procession during the Lourdes pilgrimage.

haps apply a degree of pressure that is denied to most relief agencies. The central theme though has not changed. Even when the Knights were fighting, their hospitals were a model of cleanliness and efficiency, with all patients (Our Lord's the sick, as they were called) fed off silver plates, to show them honour and because they were easily sterilised. Although the aristocratic qualifications for membership have been considerably loosened in recent times, it is no easy thing to join their ranks, and any candidate must be a practising member of the Roman Catholic Church and show the deepest commitment. The Order is still a 'religion' in every sense of the word, and full or 'professed' Knights must still take vows of poverty, chastity and obedience. However, upon installation all members vow to live their daily lives in accordance with Christian principles and obey the laws of their Church.

The 78th Prince Grand Master of the Order is Fra' Andrew Bertie, who was elected on the death of the previous Grand Master, in 1988. He is the first Englishman to head the Order since 1278. Some today think that chivalry is dead; it is not even in retreat. Many of the Orders which were founded at the time of the Crusades survive, and they fight for the survival of Christian virtues in exactly the same way as La Valette and his men did in 1565. Today, however, it is a fight against indifference and injustice, and it must be won through negotiation, handshakes and smiles. In some ways La Valette and his men had an easier time of it – the enemy was obvious and the duty clear. Whatever happens though, wherever in the world the fight goes on, one will be sure to find the Sovereign Military and Hospitaller Order of St. John of Jerusalem, of Rhodes and of Malta.

WARGAMING THE SIEGE OF MALTA

The problem with the Great Siege of Malta is that in retrospect it can seem a foregone conclusion. It seems that all the Knights need to do is keep their nerve, display their customary heroism and the highest standard of generalship and wait to be relieved.

However without the benefit of hindsight the Knights probably never saw it like that. From the bitterness of the fighting it is obvious that both sides were composed of men who acted with great courage. That of the Knights is obvious; however, how would you like to charge up a rubble ramp, made slippy with oil and blood, wearing nothing more defensive that flowing robes, to face a man in full plate armour with a deadly Elizabethan style flame thrower?

This campaign is one where there are a lot of options which have to be taken into account. Firstly, do the Turks attack Mdina first? Mustapha wanted to but was over-ruled by the perceived needs of the Fleet. I would personally not allow this option. It opens up too many possibilities and means that it is unlikely your campaign will be anything like the original. Not only that but Piali was not unreasonable in his insistence in taking the safe anchorage of Marsamuschetto. The fleet was the Turks' only means of communication. From Classical times the history of naval warfare in the western Mediterranean is one of victorious fleets being destroyed by sudden storms. If someone does insist on ignoring Piali it might be fun to have a storm blow up in early August to cause havoc on the beaches.

To play out this campaign I suggest that you photocopy the map showing the defences. Paint out the Turkish gun positions and then blow the map up until it is as large as possible. This will give you the basic ground plan to work on for refighting the siege. Once we have the map then we have to decide how we will handle the actual fighting. Personally I would go for figures on a wargames table rather than any arbitrary system. You need two things, terrain and figures. There are now several companies producing suitable siege works in a variety of scales. Making your own is also pretty easy. My favourite method is to take a strip of card as

wide as you want the height of the defences and as long as their intended frontage. Measure along the card marking off the lengths of the wall, such as between re-entrants, and then bend the card to shape. This represents the outer retaining wall. Then behind this pour thick plaster of Paris (use sand for larger scales), which represents the earth banks behind. Finally apply paint to taste. For figures it really depends upon just what you have but, the scale I would recommend 15mm, 25mm is nice but they need a lot larger scale terrain to set them off. 1/300 or 6mm is economical but I feel it is too small and impersonal for this sort of action. However, there are some nice 20mm (HO/OO) plastic figures on the market. There are Muslim troops who are not really suitable and Spanish Conquistadors who are also not totally correct. However, look at it this way, they certainly look the part, give you the feel, and are comparatively cheap, which is important because you will want to field a least a couple of hundred.

I would go for a real scale terrain with each figure representing one or two men. You need a lot of figures, but you can use simple rules and really get the feel of the action. Also it doesn't matter if you fight out the battles by yourself on a single two-feet-square terrain board with only the breach and adjacent walls, or several of you get together to build a big eight feet by six feet terrain with breach, walls and approach trenches.

Right or wrong, I would start my goal with the initial bombardment of St. Elmo on 24 May. After all, it was the Fleet's main priority. So we have to look at the effectiveness of this bombardment. It was on 29 May that the Janissaries' counterattack took the outer works of the fort. On the 30th Dragut arrived and on 6 June the ravelin was taken by coup de main. The breach was made on the 7th but it took until 23 June before the final assault succeeded. Reinforcements continued to arrive until the 20th. So if we want things to proceed as per the original it should take a month to take St. Elmo. I recommend that you formalise things here. Each day the two sides should roll a die. The Turks roll a d10 every day, the Knights a d6. This represents the bombardment and the defenders' attempts to make running repairs. Statistically there should be a difference of 1.5 per day between the two . Total up the cumulative difference. If we give the defences a defence value of 20 then statistically the defences should be breached in a couple of weeks. Each day during the bombardment, if the Turks roll a 10 and the Knights roll a 1 or 6 there is the chance of a coup de main. This means the ravelin falls without cost. However, once you have the breach you want to assault it. How do tackle the next step?

Taking part in an assault on a breach was probably the most dangerous thing you could fit into a military career. You as the player have already got your terrain and boxes full of figures, all you need to do is to fight the assault. I wouldn't limit the number of figures the players can deploy. The Turks had sheer numbers, the Knights because of the narrowness of the breach and the reinforcements they could receive from the main fortress. Because of this you can be very casual with numbers. Let the Knight player place as many figures as he wants. After all the garrison of St. Elmo was initially about 600-strong. However, the Turks can also field as many men as they want. Using a large number of figures means that you will have to use very simple rules. Something along the following lines should be suitable. You will inevitably amend them to suit your tastes, add in things such as the chance of running out of hoops or flame-throwers and similar niceties.

Defenders in cover can only be hit by missile fire if the firer rolls a 10 on a d10. I'd allow a handful of Janissary snipers who hit on a 6 on a d6. The target of Turkish fire when hit rolls a d6. Knights in their full armour are only injured on a 5 or 6. Everyone else is injured on a 3, 4, 5, 6. these injured figures are again diced for. On a 5, 6 they are dead. On a 1 or 2 they shrug it off as a scratch, otherwise they are removed from play as seriously wounded. The defenders when firing roll a d6 and hit on a 5 or 6. The target figure then rolls a d6. On a 1, 2, 3 the figure retires injured, otherwise the figure goes down, either dead or so severely wounded that he will be trampled under foot and killed by his comrades.

In close combat attackers are horribly vulnerable. Any defender using a fire weapon rolls 1d4 and that is the number of attacking figures killed. In close combat each defender rolls a d4 and kills his opponent on a 4. The attackers are badly placed being down hill and poorly armoured. They roll a d10 and kill their opponent on a roll of 10. On a

roll of 8 or 9 they drive their opponent back one and a half inches and step into his place. Perhaps Janissaries drive their opponent back on a 7, 8, or 9 and if "killed" in close combat they roll a d6 and survive on a 5 or 6. This helps take into account their greater quality and professionalism. The driving and enemy figure back one and a half inches is chosen with other ends in view, see below.

To add to everyone's misery remember how many figures were killed on the beach. (Pile this lot of dead separately.) The breach takes 1 point of slippiness for each death. Each time anyone used burning oil add 10 more points to the total. Then whenever a figure has to move more than one inch (like when they are pushed back or follow up) make then roll percentage dice. If they roll more than the current slippiness they have slipped and fallen. One hostile figure within one inch has a 50% chance of killing them without any further die rolling. This is to try to simulate the fact that the breach is going to get awfully slippy and unstable underfoot. It may also put an end point to the assault, sooner or later it will be impossible to move. When this happens the attackers will drift back (at one inch per move!) and prepare for the next wave. Each wave goes in after a notional period of reorganisation, the top of the breach is assumed to be cleared of bodies by the defenders who also want a secure footing. This assault is fought in the same manner as the last; however, the breach starts with a nominal slippiness count of 10 so it gets more treacherous faster than last time. I would limit the number of assaults per day to four.

At the end of the day you are going to have an awful lot of dead and wounded. It is also possible that the Turks have got through the breach; if they do this and get figures off the table edge with more following then obviously St. Elmo has fallen. Otherwise attrition is all. Compare dead and wounded for both sides. If the Turks' casualties are less than ten times the Knights' casualties then the Turks have cause for much rejoicing.

You cannot mount assaults day after day. Everyone needs a chance to rest, reorganise and for the attackers, point the opposition from a distance. I would say there should be a least three days between assaults.

At this point we have to take morale into consideration. Every day is hell for defenders. Indeed the assaults, if beaten off, might even be something of a relief because at least you can strike back. For the Turks faced with assaulting the breach the items in camp must seem pretty peaceful, their stress will hit them in short intense bursts. I suggest the following. Both sides start the attack on St. Elmo with a morale pool of 30 points. The defenders lose two point per day due to endless sniping and bombardment. They gain ten points if they inflict twenty times more casualties than they receive and five points if they inflict fifteen times more casualties than they receive. If they ever hit zero points they abandon the position and slip back to the main town. The Turks lose five points for every day of assault that does not take St. Elmo. If they ever get to zero then the morale of the army is called into question and the attack is abandoned. They will attack the rest of the town instead.

Sooner or later there will be an end to the St. Elmo fighting. At this point it will be time to start on either Birgu or Senglia. You can use the same system. Both sides start with 60 morale points. If the Turks abandoned the attack on St. Elmo they start on 50 instead. As the Bombardment was not as fierce as it had been on St. Elmo the Knights only lose one point per day due to its effects. Also due to the difficulty in getting supplies and the raids from the Knights' cavalry, the Turks lose four points a week, all of which are lost on Thursday. Roll the dice every day for each side for the bombardment and try to overcome the enemy's morale with assaults. The Turks can try other things that weren't possible against St. Elmo, boatloads of troops attacking across the water, siege towers and mines. I would say that whereas when attacking St. Elmo you had a chance of *coup de main* and taking the ravelin, facing either Birgu or Senglia and rolling a *coup de main* means that you have managed to get a siege tower in place. This will take pride of place on the wargames table during the next assault. Mines have to be factored in differently. I would use playing cards. The Turks need red cards, the Knights black. Each day deal a card face down to each player. The Turk wants to dig a tunnel of five red cards, whilst the Knights want to find it and fill it in. To do this they will put together a countermine of five black cards. When the Turk thinks he has his tunnel he shall announce it, the Knight must immediately play his counter mine. All you do is treat the cards as poker hands with the highest one winning. If the Turks win they have successfully exploded the mine, if the Knights win then they have successfully countermined.

If the mine is successful the wall has been breached and an assault can be mounted. The Turks immediately gain five morale points for successfully blowing the mine, the Knights lose five morale points due to the casualties and confusion caused. Should the Knights' morale ever drop to zero then they will ask for terms. If the Turks' morale is below 30 they will grant them. If the Turks' morale is above 30 they will demand unconditional surrender. The Knights can now go down to a morale of minus 10 before their morale cracks irrevocably and the siege is over.

The siege drags on waiting for one side or another to crack. The next thing to look at is the final relief. The Little Relief I haven't included as a separate episode, I tried to factor it into the overall morale. Actually it would make a nice mini campaign in its own right. Finally the relief force lands on 6 September. Here I would say that on 1 September the umpire of 'Knights' player rolls a ten-sided die and the number is the date the relief force lands. So, a one means that it lands on the first, it just adds slightly to the uncertainty. If the Turks' morale has already dropped to zero they will have already left. If it is less than five they will flee to their ships when the relief force lands. If their morale is between five and 15 they will make a sudden counter-attack, however, most of their troops should be treated as Horde and only the Janissaries should have any military value. If the Turks' morale is over 15 then it is the usual competent Turkish army that you must defeat.

With these wargaming suggestions I have tried to give you something which will take you through the Great Siege of Malta and which is recognisable as the historical siege. There are many other options. A nice little campaign would be to take the Knights' force at Mdina and have them acting as partisans, attacking the overstretched Turkish lines. Another interesting scenario would be to try to produce wargames rules for Maltese and Turkish swimmers and boat crews in the water trying to remove the Senglia's palisade of stakes. I can see that being a fascinating little game. Either way I hope you find something here of interest, I've tried to stick to the historical campaign but not to lead you by the nose into making historical mistakes. Refighting this siege will be a major project but sieges were and tended to be won by attrition. Fight it out to a conclusion and you should at least get a sense of achievement, whether you win or lose.

Firing Table

FIRER	TARGET	DIE ROLL NEEDED TO HIT
Ordinary Turk	Defender	10 on a d10
Janissary Sniper	Defender	6 on a d6
Defender	Attacker	5,6 on a d6

TARGET	DICE ROLL TO SAVE IF HIT	RESULT IF HIT
Knight	1, 2, 3, 4 on a d6	5, 6 dead, 3, 4 wounded. 1, 2 irrelevant scratch
Other Defenders	1, 2 on a d6	5, 6 dead, 3, 4 wounded. 1, 2 irrelevant scratch
Attackers	No save	1, 2, 3 wounded. 4, 5, 6 dead

Close Combat Table

COMBATANT	ROLL TO HIT	OTHER RESULTS
Christian using fire weapon against everyone	d4. This gives the number of casualties	None
Christian with other weapons against all but Janissaries	4 on d4 kills	None
Christian with other weapons against Janissaries	4 on d4 kills	Janissary rolls d6. On 5, 6 is not killed but is driven back
Turks	10 on a d10	8, 9 on a d10 drive opponent back
Janissaries	10 on a d10	7, 8, 9 on d10 drive opponent back

Morale

At this point we have to take morale into consideration. Every day is hell for defenders. Indeed the assaults, if beaten off, might even be something of a relief because at least you can strike back. For the Turks faced with assaulting the breach the items in camp must seem pretty peaceful, their stress will hit them in short intense bursts. I suggest the following.

FACTORS AFFECTING POINTS	TURKS	CHRISTIANS
Start the play with	+30	+30
Each day		-2
Each day with an assault	-5	
Each week without an assault		+5
Inflict x20 casualities than receive	—	+10
Inflict x 15 casualities than receive	—	+5

If they ever hit zero points they abandon the position and slip back to the main town. If they ever get to zero then the morale of the entire army is called into question a and the attack is abandoned. They will attack the rest of the town instead.

Slippage

To add to everyone's misery remember how many figures were killed on the beach. (Pile this lot of dead separately).

FACTORS AFFECTING SLIPPAGE	POINTS
Each death	+1
Using burning oil	+10
Each assault	+10

I would limit the number of assaults per day to four

INDEX

(References to illustrations are shown in bold)